THE YOUNG DETECTIVE'S HANDBOOK

THE YOUNG DETECTIVE'S HANDBOOK

William Vivian Butler

Illustrated by
Lucinda Landon

The Atlantic Monthly Press
BOSTON   NEW YORK

Library of Congress Cataloging in Publication Data

Butler, William Vivian, 1927–
  The young detective's handbook.

  "An Atlantic Monthly Press book."
  Summary: Introduces aspiring detectives to the
fundamentals of criminal investigation. Includes
games and activities to develop skill in fingerprinting, interpreting clues, organizing investigations, making deductions, and using secret
messages, codes, and disguises.
    1. Detectives—Juvenile literature.
  [1. Detectives.   2. Criminal investigation]
  I. Landon, Lucinda, ill.   II. Title.
  HV8073.8.B87   1981   363.2'5   81-11753
                                           AACR2

  ISBN 0-87113-060-2

BP

PRINTED IN THE UNITED STATES OF AMERICA

To
MARY
with all my love
— BILL

Contents

THE YOUNG DETECTIVE'S HANDBOOK

INTRODUCTION

Heroes All

ALL through history, most human beings have se-
cretly wanted to be heroes. But it's only in the past
ninety years or so that millions of people have wanted
to be a certain kind of hero: a brilliant detective.

Here's how the whole thing began. Back in the
days of gaslight and hansom cabs — in the early 1890s
— a hard-up London doctor named Arthur Conan
Doyle began writing stories about an imaginary private detective, a certain Mr. Sherlock Holmes.

Holmes wasn't the first detective in fiction. That
honor belongs to C. Auguste Dupin, created around
1840 by the American writer Edgar Allan Poe. But
Sherlock Holmes was the first to be really popular —
and that's putting it mildly.

Each month, a new Sherlock Holmes story used to
come out in a journal called *The Strand Magazine*.
My father was a boy at the time, and for the rest of
his life, he never forgot the excitement of standing in

line outside his local bookstore trying to get a copy. Everyone was so eager to be the first to read the latest Holmes adventure, that most months, he told me, the line of would-be *Strand*-buyers stretched five times around the block! I don't think that any other series of stories has ever created such a sensation, before or since.

You may never have read a Holmes story, or seen any of the hundred or more films that have been made about him. But even so, I'll bet that as soon as you saw the name "Sherlock Holmes," you had a picture of him in your mind's eye — a tall, aloof individual with a thin, hawklike face, smoking a large curved pipe, peering at clues through a magnifying glass, and accompanied everywhere by his dazed and admiring friend, Dr. Watson. Holmes wasn't a particularly pleasant character. He could be cold, conceited, and irritable. He was so fond of showing off his cleverness that frequently, he got on even Watson's nerves. But there was a strange magic about him, and you could say that the world is still under his spell — particularly the English-speaking world.

In the ninety years since *The Adventures of Sherlock Holmes* appeared, there have been literally hundreds of British and American detective heroes, and each has had an army of fans. To begin with, the heroes were direct copies of Sherlock Holmes. When I was a boy, I used to hurry to *my* local bookstore to buy *Detective Weekly*. Week after week for thirty years, this magazine had been featuring Sexton Blake, who was — surprise, surprise! — a tall, aloof, hawklike character with a curved briar pipe and a magnifying glass always at the ready. But my favorite reading in those days was a paper called *The Thriller*, which introduced me to a very different hero, who has since become equally famous on both sides of the Atlantic. He was a dashing modern Robin Hood called Simon Templar, alias The Saint, who not only chased villains but was all the time hotly pursued by Chief Inspector Teal of Scotland Yard. (Scotland Yard, just in case you didn't know, is the headquarters of the London police force. It is often made fun of in British thrillers, but is in real life one of the most advanced police centers in the world.)

At about the same time that English kids like me were reading about Sexton Blake and The Saint, American boys and girls were eagerly following the great comic strip detective heroes Dick Tracy and Batman. Tracy was a clean-jawed city cop who fought gangsters, rather in the Kojak style. Batman was tall, dignified, and very much more Holmes-like — except that he was a brilliant acrobat, a master at climbing walls and leaping from roof to roof. He was also very much less irritable than Holmes. In fact, he and his boy assistant, Robin, remain calm and smiling in the face of attacks by the weirdest collection of arch-criminals in thriller history (Catwoman, to give just one example). Perhaps I should also include Superman, but since he came from another planet and had X-ray eyes, it's hardly fair to compare him with Earth-born detectives.

For people who liked to read a bit more than just

the balloons in comic strips, there were now an incredible number of thriller heroes on the American scene. There were the tough guys — like Sam Spade and Philip Marlowe (think of Humphrey Bogart in a slouch hat and a raincoat, and you'll have a pretty good idea of what they were like). There was the world's most famous criminal attorney, Perry Mason. No one could beat him at making stirring courtroom speeches and coming up with the vital clue in the nick of time to stop his client from being jailed for ninety-nine years. There was the staggeringly fat Nero Wolfe, weighing one seventh of a ton, who had such difficulty heaving himself out of his chair that he solved most of his cases without leaving his home. He just folded his hands across his stomach, closed his eyes, and used his brain! By contrast, there was Ellery Queen, an energetic but very untidy young man, who had such a quick mind that he solved in a flash most of the problems bothering his harassed father, Inspector Richard Queen of the New York police. In movies, there was the crime-solving society couple, Nick and Nora Charles, with their almost equally clever dog, Asta — and Charlie Chan, a Chinaman who never opened his mouth without a motto coming out of it. ("Clue like treasure buried in snow: sooner or later it come to surface").

English detectives with millions of U.S. fans included Lord Peter Wimsey, a lounging aristocrat whose eye missed nothing, once he had screwed a monocle into it; Miss Jane Marple, a prim old lady who solved crimes in quaint English villages, and then calmly went on with her needlework; and Hercule Poirot, a little Belgian with a waxed mustache who was always boasting about the power of "the little grey cells" in his brain. Miss Marple and Poirot were the inventions of Agatha Christie, the cleverest author in the world at lining up a collection of suspects, and then challenging the reader to spot "whodunit." Meanwhile, on the radio, there was The Shadow — the weirdest detective of them all, who had hypnotic powers and could make himself invisible whenever he wanted!

In more recent times, there have been famous television detective heroes — Columbo, Kojak, Charlie's Angels, even the Hardy Boys. In books and in films, the greatest hero since the war, of course, has been James Bond. Although he's really a spy and not a detective, he's no slouch when it comes to following clues — in fact, his very survival usually depends on it. And John le Carré's quiet, rather sinister Secret Service head, George Smiley, is so clever and subtle that he has become the favorite hero of the smartest detective story fans in both America and Britain. Meanwhile, for boys and girls who prefer detective heroes and heroines who are their own age, there are plenty of brilliant ones around, like Nancy Drew, the Hardy Boys, and Encyclopedia Brown.

That's about thirty detectives I've mentioned. I could easily go on to list a hundred more. But all of them, from the vast Nero Wolfe to the invisible Shadow, from quaint old Miss Marple to pretty young Nancy Drew, have one thing in common with

Sherlock Holmes. They notice things — often tiny, seemingly unimportant things — that other people miss. And that's an ability they share with the best real-life detectives, all over the world.

Whether you ask the FBI or Scotland Yard — or, for that matter, the French Sûreté — they'll tell you the same thing. In the end, it isn't *guns* that beat criminals. It's *brains* — the ability to spot clues, and follow them.

If you wish you could develop this ability, then you've come to the right place. This book is here to show you how. There are no limits to the intriguing things that can happen once you start following in the footsteps — or perhaps I should say, the footprints — of the great detectives of fiction — and fact.

Those prints start here.

CHAPTER 1

You—Crime-Spotter

1. HOW TO BEGIN

There is only one way I can start this book and that is with a warning.

In this chapter and the ones that follow, you can discover how to play a real part in fighting crime; what to watch out for; what (and what not) to report to the police; how to have fun with detection — including how to start a detective club, how to outfit yourself as a detective, how to take fingerprints and collect clues, how to send secret messages, how to make up codes and decipher enemy ones, how to make Sherlock Holmes–type deductions, and how to disguise yourself as a completely different person. Finally, you can learn how to be a crime-prevention expert — and how to start training yourself to be as hawk-eyed as any real detective.

There is one thing that is more important than all the rest, and that's the thing you have to learn first.

Otherwise, it would be better to forget about being a young detective altogether.

Rule One.

If you come up against any sort of real-life crime — in school or out of it — don't make ANY attempt to investigate. Just observe, and (if it's serious enough) report.

It's a commonsense rule, really. These days, there are all kinds of criminals about, and it could be very dangerous if you tried to meddle in any of their affairs on your own.

And don't forget: a lot of these criminals are young. Forty percent of all persons arrested in the U.S. in 1979 were under 21, twenty-three percent under 18 and seven percent under 15. So even if you start to investigate a small-scale incident at school on your own (say, bicycle tires being deflated) before you know it, you could find yourself surrounded by a gang of other kids, or getting beaten up on the way home.

That's not the kind of thing I like to happen to my readers. They're not usually too eager to buy my next book.

Seriously, please remember: detecting for fun is one thing, investigating in earnest is quite another. The only safe way to help beat real crime is to:

1. Keep your eyes open. (Which includes, of course, making *deductions* about what you see.)

2. Carry a notebook and pencil in your pocket, ready to write down the exact details of anything suspicious.

3. Get your parents to call the police — or in an

Three Young Detectives

emergency, contact the police yourself — whenever you really believe you're on to something important.

2. AN EIGHT-YEAR-OLD CAPTURES BANK ROBBERS

In case you feel that you can't do much to catch crooks that way, here are some true stories, told recently by Shaw Taylor in England. *Junior Police 5*, a TV program run with the help of Scotland Yard, was watched by millions of children — all of whom were asked to follow the rules listed above. These children called themselves "*Junior Police 5* Observers."

One day, an eight-year-old girl strode into a London police station and calmly informed the sergeant at the desk:

"I'm a *Junior Police 5* Observer. I've just seen three men acting suspiciously."

The sergeant smiled patronizingly.

"Have you, now? And what were they up to?"

"Nothing," said the eight-year-old. "It's just that they've been sitting in a car in the same place for the past half-hour."

She produced her notebook and told the sergeant —
- (a) The exact place where the car was parked,
- (b) The make of the car,
- (c) The color of the car, and
- (d) Its license plate.

By that time, the sergeant's smile was no longer quite so patronizing.

"Good work," he said. "I'll check that out."

Police stations all over Britain share what is called the National Police Computer. The sergeant picked up the phone, dialed Scotland Yard, and asked to be put through to the computer room. Then he read out the details the girl had given him, and these were fed into the computer.

Within seconds, the computer had come back with the information that the car was a stolen one.

The sergeant didn't waste any time after that. He contacted the inspector in charge of the police station, and a couple of minutes later, two police cars, with six men in each, were rushing to the spot where the little girl had said the car was waiting.

The spot turned out to be opposite a bank where a large amount of cash was due to be delivered.

The men sitting in the car were taken completely by surprise. Before they realized what was happening, they found themselves surrounded by policemen, and under arrest.

There is no doubt that if the police hadn't arrived when they did, a serious holdup would have taken place; thousands of dollars would have been stolen, and very possibly several people injured or killed.

All this was prevented because an eight-year-old girl used her eyes, and her notebook — and took care to get ALL the facts.

There's another reason why I admire that girl. She somehow succeeded in writing all those things down *without the men in the car noticing her looking at them.* Crime-spotters have to be very skillful at not being spotted themselves. I imagine this girl was sharp-eyed enough to take in everything more or less at a glance; then she must have run around a corner and scribbled it all down once she was safely out of sight.

Crime-Spotter at Work

3. A CAPTURE BY MOVIE CAMERA

Of course, if you happen to have a movie camera handy, and are a safe distance away, it's a lot better than a notebook. A couple of years ago a seventeen-year-old schoolgirl was looking out of her bedroom window, when she saw two men climbing through the window of an old people's home.

She grabbed a movie camera (being lucky enough to have one near), turned it on to the two men, and actually filmed the whole break-in! Because of this, the police were able to identify the burglars — and the judge awarded that girl $50 for her "very substantial" help in the case.

4. A NEW USE FOR A PAVEMENT

But without a notebook or camera, remembering important details can be very difficult indeed. Shaw Taylor also tells the story of a group of children who were playing tag in the street, when one of them climbed up a wall to get away from a boy who was chasing him. From the top of the wall he spotted two men breaking open a garage door with crowbars. He waved to the other children to come and watch too. Eventually, there were five or six children all on top of the wall, watching the crooks go into the garage, and start to load stolen tires into a truck.

Now, none of those children had a notebook, a pen, or even a piece of paper. They had to keep repeating the license number of the truck under their breath. When the crooks had gone, they jumped down from the wall and, using a piece of stone, scrawled the number on the pavement.

It worked, mind you. The police came and read the number off the pavement, and as a result, the crooks were duly caught. But you've got to admit — pavements make rather cumbersome notebooks. And what on earth would those kids have done if all this had happened in a field? (Though there is a good trick for memorizing the alphabet part of license numbers. Turn the letters into names in your mind — "CDH" becoming "Charlie Dave Harry" and so on. You'll find them twice as easy to remember then.)

5. WHAT TO WATCH OUT FOR

Walking along the street . . . looking out of your own bedroom window . . . playing tag . . . you never know when or where you might suddenly find yourself seeing something suspicious.

You might, like that girl in London, see a group of men — perhaps a single man — loitering about outside a bank or shop. Or a house where you know the owners are away. You might be walking home with some friends down a dark road at night and hear a suspicious sound — perhaps breaking glass — coming from the back of a house.*

You might hear a knock on your front door, and when you open it, see a man turning and running

* You have to use your common sense, of course. The sound might be just the owner of the house dropping bottles into the garbage!

away. (This happened to my son a few years ago. Obviously the man was a would-be thief who, for some reason or other, had imagined that there was nobody at home.)

Or you might see a car charging along at reckless speed. (Very often, that could be a crook escaping, so it's always worth taking down its number.) Or you might spot a strange car in your neighborhood, which no one seems to own. Chances are that it's been abandoned by some criminal, and should be reported without delay.

In other words, you never know when you might bump into a crime. That's why it's so important always to have a notebook and pencil handy.

6. WHAT TO WRITE DOWN

These are the things you should note:

1. *The time.* If you've got a watch, write it exactly. (Not just "around two," but 2:07, 2:18 or whatever.)

2. *The place.* Don't just put the name of the street — some streets are several miles long! — but the number of the nearest house, the name of the nearest shop, anything which will identify the exact spot you mean.

3. If a car is involved, you should note color, make, and license number. Also whether there is anything damaged on the car — if a bumper or door is dented, for example — and if there are any special identifying stickers on the windows or bumpers.

4. If people are involved, write a very quick de-

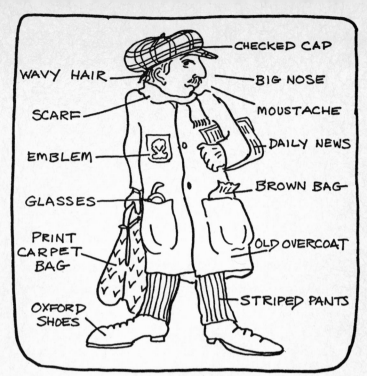

What to Remember

scription of each suspect, mentioning things like:

Height. The easiest way of reckoning this is by noticing how much *taller than you* the person is.

Build. This really means whether the person is fat or thin.

Color of eyes — and whether he or she is wearing glasses.

Color of hair — and if it's thick or thinning.

Complexion — pale, red-faced, freckled, spotty, etc.

Clothing. In the case of a man, color of coat, suit, shirt, tie, trousers, shoes, etc. In the case of a woman, color of dress, skirt, blouse, pants, shoes, etc.

And finally — try to say what the person's face looks like. I know that's quite a tall order; faces are extremely difficult to describe.

But here are a few things to look out for:

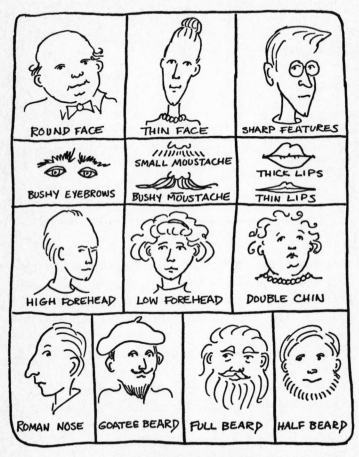

ROUND FACE

THIN FACE

SHARP FEATURES

BUSHY EYEBROWS

SMALL MOUSTACHE

BUSHY MOUSTACHE

THICK LIPS

THIN LIPS

HIGH FOREHEAD

LOW FOREHEAD

DOUBLE CHIN

ROMAN NOSE

GOATEE BEARD

FULL BEARD

HALF BEARD

Telltale Facial Characteristics

And always note down any *peculiarities* about a suspect whom you may happen to spot — especially peculiarities that may be hard to disguise, such as a mole on the cheek, a scar on the back of the hand, a tattoo on the wrist, a broken nose, a habit of wrinkling the forehead when talking, unusually large ears, a squint, a pronounced limp: any little detail like that can become an important clue.

Of course, it's very easy to make a list of things you *ought* to put in your notebook. In the actual event, though, you'll be excited. You'll probably find it hard to scrawl more than a few words. But however difficult it may be, do try to get down as much as you possibly can while the memory of what happened is still clear in your mind.

Remember, there is all the difference in the world between saying you saw a "funny-looking man just now hanging about somewhere down the end of High Street" and being able to state that at 6:17 P.M., you witnessed a tall, round-faced man with bushy eyebrows and a broken nose trying the door of a closed Lord and Taylor's. If you could add that he was wearing a raincoat and a blue-and-white scarf; that he limped as he walked; and that he made off in a bright red Ford sedan, license no. S40 7443, you'll have been as good a witness as a police officer, and probably even Sherlock Holmes couldn't have done much better!

7. CONTACTING THE POLICE

Let's say, then, that you've spotted something suspicious going on. You've taken a good look — preferably out of the corner of your eye. You've run around the corner, well out of sight of the suspect. You've whipped out a notebook, and written down the time, the place, and as many facts as you can remember.

What happens next?

Well, if you're near home, the sensible thing to do is to run there as quickly as you can, and ask your parents to telephone the police.

If you're a long way from home — and you believe a crime is likely to be committed very soon — then your best course is to call the police yourself from a pay phone. You'll find their number in the telephone book (under P for police, of course) or you can dial "Operator" and ask for the police. The call shouldn't cost you more than 10¢.

Eagle Eyes

But in a real emergency (say, if you've actually seen some vandals smashing a shop window, or heard someone yell for help, or anything like that) there is no need to use any coins at all. You simply go to the pay phone, pick up the receiver, and dial 911 or "Operator." A voice will ask you whether you want the fire, police or ambulance services. You just have to say one word — "Police" — and you'll be connected right away.

Of course, emergency or not, if you happen to be near a police station, there's no harm in walking straight in to have a talk with the sergeant at the desk.

You needn't feel shy about doing so.

He may smile patronizingly at you when you go in. But once you bring out your notebook, and start giving him precise facts, he'll treat you — and your story — with the seriousness it deserves.

And as long as it *is* a story that deserves to be taken seriously, something rather important will have happened to you.

You'll have started to make the grade as a young detective.

By this time, there is one question which I am sure you are dying to ask.

Let's say that you've decided to become a young detective, and you're trying hard. You've got into the habit of carrying a notebook and pencil. You've read and reread all the things you ought to watch out for. You've learned by heart all the things you ought to write down. You've studied the sketches of faces until you feel you could tell a high forehead from a low one even across a street.

But suppose that day after day goes by, and you don't see anything remotely resembling a crime.

What do you do then?

There's a very simple answer to that.

You go on to the next page, and start *Detecting for Fun.*

Ready for Action!

CHAPTER 2

Detecting for Fun— Equipment

1. FORMING A YOUNG DETECTIVES' CLUB

Before you can become good at anything in this life, you need constant practice — and being a good detective is no exception.

The best way to get the practice you need is to rope in some of your friends, and form a YDC — a Young Detectives' Club.

To qualify for membership, each person has to promise to firmly and fervently fight all kinds of crime and crookedness. You will need to carry a notebook and pencil at all times, and to assemble a —

2. SCENE-OF-THE-CRIME KIT

This kit is essential to detecting for fun if you want your games to be realistic. Real-life investigations always begin with a close examination of the scene of the crime. And just as a doctor carries a little black bag containing a stethoscope, thermometer, and other medical equipment, so a detective takes a scene-of-the-crime kit with him to every inquiry.

The kit below is based on the one the Scotland Yard experts use, and yet I don't believe you'll find it all that difficult to assemble.

You will need:

1. A notebook and pencil (or pen). Essential both for detecting for fun and crime-spotting.

2. A magnifying-glass. The detective's trademark — and very, very useful for examining anything from a scratch to a thumbprint.

Tools of the Trade

3. Fingerprint powder. You can make this yourself for very little money. Just buy one or two blocks of charcoal from any art supplies shop: they cost around ten cents each. Scratch at one of these blocks with a penknife just as though you were sharpening a pencil. In a couple of seconds you'll have a sizable heap of powder. But watch your clothes — it's hard stuff to get off a shirt or sweater.

There are, incidentally, many other powders you could use — but most contain harmful chemicals, and are best avoided. Charcoal powder is not only harmless; it is so effective that it is one of the main tools in every Scotland Yard fingerprint expert's kit. It works well on most surfaces — particularly metal, glass, or paper. You can use it, too, on desktops or floorboards, although even Yard men reckon that you have to be lucky to get a good fingerprint from wood, unless it happens to be polished. On a very dark surface, the fingerprints may not show up too well, and it is best to make the charcoal powder gray instead of black by mixing it with a little dressmaker's (or even crushed blackboard) chalk.

4. An artist's small paintbrush (paintbox type — not the kind you use for house decorating!) for applying the fingerprint powder.

5. A pair of tweezers for picking up small clues, such as stray hairs, particles of fabric, etc.

6. A roll of transparent tape for taping fingerprints — see page 28.

7. A packet of small envelopes for putting taped fingerprints and other small clues in.

8. Five or six very large envelopes for the more sizable clues.

9. A piece of blackboard chalk. As soon as you spot what might be a clue — say, a faint smudge or a thumbprint — it's a good idea to draw an arrow pointing to it, so that you can find it easily again. You have to be careful, of course, that in chalking the arrows, you don't step on or obscure other clues that might be close by.

10. Sheets of tracing paper, for tracing footprints, tire tracks — anything that is too big to be captured on transparent tape.

11. A tape measure. You never know when measurements may be essential.

12. A flashlight. Sometimes you need to look for clues under ledges or in dark corners.

13. A pocket knife or pair of scissors for cutting tape.

And finally, of course:

14. A box to contain all the above items — although, in fact, they are small enough to fit into a large envelope, if you prefer.

Now that you're equipped, the next stage is to get some practice in the trickiest part of amateur detective work: fingerprinting.

I ought to start by saying that fingerprinting isn't really an amateur's game at all. It is a highly expert science; the police themselves leave it to their own trained specialists.

Nevertheless, as I've proved myself, even the most

bungling amateur *can* get exciting results if he keeps trying — and has a bit of beginner's luck.

3. BRINGING UP FINGERPRINTS

The first thing to do is choose an object which you think a lot of people have recently handled. It doesn't matter what the object is: a glass, a wastepaper basket, a transistor radio, a pocket calculator, a model airplane, even an old envelope will do. (As a matter of fact, charcoal powder works particularly well on paper.) You could always pass the object among your friends to make sure it's well fingerprinted before you start.

Now get out your fingerprint powder and paintbrush, and gently brush the powder over the outside surfaces of the object. (In the case of the radio and pocket calculator, make sure none of it gets inside, to gum up the works!)

You will be surprised how many marks appear that were invisible before. A lot of those marks will be blurry smudges. Probably they will *all* look like blurry smudges at first. But when you examine them under your magnifying glass, you will very likely find that among those marks will be thumbprints or fingerprints.

Once a print has appeared, you can make it sharper by very gently working over and around it with the brush, to clear away the surplus powder. A print is called "sharp" when you can begin to count the "ridges" — the tiny lines on it — without straining your eyes.

4. TAPING FINGERPRINTS

At this stage, the police experts would normally start photographing the print with a camera with a flash-bulb attachment, so that they can send it to Scotland Yard's Records Department for comparing with the millions of "wanted men and women" prints in their files.

You can't do anything like that, of course. Even if you have a camera, film is very expensive, and finger-prints are very hard to photograph. What's more, they don't make very entertaining pictures! A far simpler — and cheaper — method of keeping prints is to use a strip of clear adhesive tape.

If you lay the tape across the powdered print, sticky side down, the print will transfer to the tape; and if you hold the tape up to the light and look at it through a magnifying glass, you will find that the print will show up as clearly as any photograph.

But if you put the "taped" print into a clues en-velope as it is, the tape will stick to the inside of the envelope, and the print will be lost. So, take a *second* strip of tape and press it on top of the first (putting the sticky sides of both tapes together). In that way, you'll have the fingerprint neatly caught between two pieces of tape, and can put it in an envelope with absolutely no risk at all of losing it.

5. YOUR OWN FINGERPRINT DOSSIER

Identifying fingerprints is once again an exact science — but here too, there's no reason why you shouldn't have a stab at it with some success.

As everyone knows, no two people have fingerprints that are exactly alike. And very often, they aren't *at all* alike. For one thing, fingers vary a great deal in size — and so, naturally, do prints. (To start with, girls normally have smaller prints than boys.) For another thing, if you compare prints belonging to different people under a magnifying glass, you will find that each has a different pattern of "ridges" and "whorls."

Examples of two different fingerprints, dusted with charcoal powder. The lines across are called "ridges" and the circular bits "whorls." Under a magnifying glass, it's quite easy to detect big pattern-differences. Yard experts usually count the actual number of "ridges" which usually varies widely from print to print.

Using this system, it shouldn't be too difficult to discover whose prints you've taped — although, in the process, you'll probably have to take the fingerprints of a lot of your friends for comparison.

No Two are Alike

As a matter of fact, I would suggest that every member of your YDC compiles a dossier of club fingerprints. Here's how to do it.

Take a long strip of adhesive tape, and then fix to the bottom of it — for labeling purposes — an equally long strip of paper, about ¼ inch or 5 millimeters wide.

Lay the tape on your desk, sticky side up. Pile up a mound of fingerprint powder beside it.

Then dip your own fingers into the powder and place the tips of them onto the beginning of the strip of tape (sticky side, of course). Don't forget to do your thumbprints, too. When you've taped all ten of your own prints, take a pen and label them by writing underneath them on the labeling strip.

Now ask all of the other members of your club to put their prints on the tape too, so that you wind up with complete sets of their fingerprints and thumbprints, all neatly labeled — for example: "Ron (left

hand) . . . Ron (right hand) . Sue (left hand) . . ."
and so on.

Then take a second strip of tape and press it against the first. This captures the prints between two layers of tape, as explained earlier.

I said you would need a long strip of tape. If your club has five or six members, you could come close to using up a whole roll. But it will be worth it. You'll possess a complete fingerprint dossier of your club; and you can invite each of the other members to do one too.

You are now ready to attempt a very intriguing Detective Club exercise, called —

6. THE "WHO TOUCHED IT" GAME

An object — an ashtray, a metal ruler, anything that will take good fingerprints — is carefully wiped with a handkerchief and then placed on the floor in the center of the room.

A member of the club is chosen to be the Detective and is sent out of the room, but within hearing distance.

The remaining members of the club choose someone to be the Crook.

The rest of the exercise is very straightforward.

1. The Crook picks up the object.

2. The others shout "Stop, Thief!" but otherwise, nobody moves or speaks.

3. The Crook drops the object and hurriedly joins the crowd.

4. The Detective, hearing the shout, rushes back into the room.

5. He picks up the object and, with the help of fingerprint powder, paintbrush, magnifying glass, sticky tape, etc., tries to find and tape the Crook's fingerprints.

6. The Detective then has to compare the fingerprint with the others in his Club Dossier, and decide which member of the club is the Crook.

7. The Detective is given a time limit — say, ten minutes — in which to do his fingerprint work and announce his Suspect No. 1.

8. If he's right, he gets 10 points. If he's wrong, everyone else gets 2 points and the Crook 5.

I can't guarantee that you'll find this an easy exercise. But I do believe it will prove highly entertaining — and any "Detective" who succeeds in identifying the "Crook" from his (or her) fingerprints will have the satisfaction of knowing that he has equaled the Scotland Yard fingerprint experts at their own highly expert game.

If that isn't good detective work, what is?

CHAPTER 3

Detecting for Fun—Clues

1. THE BIG CLUE RULE

Fingerprints are, of course, only one of many kinds of clues that you are likely to come across in amateur detection. This chapter suggests games or activities that will give you valuable practice in dealing with clues of every description.

But first of all, there's one important rule about clues which you should always remember. However big or small a clue — whether it's a foot-square tracing of a bicycle tire track or a microscopic bit of fluff — a good detective will always treat it with the utmost care.

Let's say you find the torn half of a bus ticket under a desk and, for some reason, you think that this is an important clue. Now if you were to put that ticket into, say, the back pocket of your jeans, all possible fingerprints on it would be rubbed off in two seconds flat. And if you were just to shove it into your wallet, it could easily get mixed up with the other things you've got in there, and end up battered, torn, or lost.

The only sensible thing to do with this — or any similar clue — is to:

(a) Examine it with a magnifying glass and make sure that it *is* important;

(b) Pick it up with a pair of tweezers;

(c) Slip it into an envelope, and

(d) Write on the outside of the envelope the spot where it was found, the time at which you found it, and the date. Like this:

TORN HALF OF BUS TICKET FOUND UNDER GORDON MATTHEW'S DESK IN CLASS 4A, 12:45 P.M., 10/4/81.

The Young Detectives' Club

There may not be time to do this in all the activities suggested in this chapter. But it's still a good idea, whenever possible, to handle clues with tweezers, and have envelopes ready to pop them in.

Otherwise, don't blame me if you suddenly find that you haven't a clue.

2. THE "CARELESS CROOK" GAME

The next three games are really alternative versions of the "Who Touched It" game suggested in Chapter 2.

They all start the same way. Someone is chosen as the Detective and asked to go out of the room — and preferably at least twenty paces down the corridor. Then, the remaining members of the club pick one of their number to be the Crook.

In the "Who Touched It" game all the Crook had to do was leave his or her fingerprints on an object.

In the "Careless Crook" game the Crook has to do very much more.

A certain area of the room is chosen to be the "Scene of the Crime," and chalk marks are drawn all around it. This shouldn't be a very large area — 4 feet square at the most. That's about enough to accommodate a school desk and the chair behind it.

While all the other members of the club stand and watch, the Crook then has to leave *at least five clues* in the "Scene of the Crime" area.

The clues must all be different. (Fingerprints, even if the Crook leaves them all over the place, still only count as one clue.) And each clue must be fair: in other words, it must be a reasonable pointer to the Crook's identity.

For example, let's suppose the Crook is a girl called Beryl Simms; that she has long brown hair, and is wearing a bright green sweater. She could leave:

1. Her fingerprints on top of the desk.
2. A strand of wool from her sweater on the seat of the chair.
3. A couple of strands of hair just beside it.
4. The wrapper from a bar of chocolate on the floor beside the chair.
5. The top of her ball-point pen underneath the chair.

She then asks the other members of the club if they think these clues are fair (their majority verdict is final). The club would agree that they *are* fair — provided that:

1. Beryl's ball-point pen isn't exactly the same as anyone else's in the class.
2. The bar of chocolate really is a kind that Beryl is known to eat often.

Otherwise, the club should insist that Beryl leave a stronger clue — say, a charm bracelet with B on it or a comb.

Once the club has decided that five fair clues have been left, Beryl leaves the "Scene of the Crime" area and becomes a seemingly innocent bystander, and the Detective is called into the room.

He or she is shown the "Scene of the Crime" area, and is allowed five minutes to go over it with a mag-

Careless Clues

nifying glass, flashlight, fingerprint powder, and so on. (The Detective is allowed to use any item in his Scene-of-the-Crime Kit.) At the end of the five minutes, the Detective has to name the Crook.

If he does this successfully, he scores 10 points. But he has to explain his reasoning, and if he has simply made a lucky guess and not followed any clue he only scores 5. If he names the wrong person, then of course it is the Crook who scores 10.

3. THE "TELLTALE FOOTPRINT" GAME

This is an outdoor version of the "Who Touched It" game, which can be played on any stretch of concrete, but not, of course, on a road. In this game, the Detective can't, obviously, go out of the room. Instead, he or she should walk fifty paces away from the rest, preferably around a corner. And the Crook, instead of leaving fingerprints, leaves *footprints*.

As soon as the Detective has left and the Crook has been chosen, the Crook wets the soles of his or her shoes — if it's been raining, by stepping into a shallow puddle; if it's dry, by pouring some water on the concrete and walking over the wet patch. All the other members of the club should then wet their shoes in the same way. (Otherwise, the returning Detective would immediately spot who'd done it — he'd only have to look and see who had wet shoes!)

The object to be stolen — an outdoor object this time, say a football or a baseball bat — is placed in the middle of the concrete area. The members of the club form a circle around the object. The Crook has to walk across and snatch it, leaving footprints all the way.

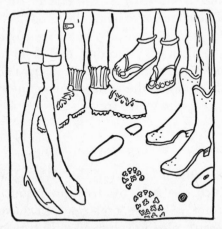

The Tell-tale Footprint

As in the "Who Touched It" game, the others shout "Stop, Thief!" The Crook drops the object and runs to join the others before the Detective's return. (Everyone will have to do a certain amount of shuffling around the circle at this point. Otherwise the wet footprints will lead the Detective straight to the Crook.)

The Detective then has five minutes to examine the footprints through his magnifying glass; to take tracings of them, measure them, or whatever he wants to do with them. During this five minutes, he can ask anybody in the Club to lift up their feet — one at a time, of course — and allow the Detective to examine the soles and heels of their shoes. The Detective can take measurements of soles and heels, but is not allowed to remove anyone's shoe.

When the five minutes are up, the Detective, of course, has to name the Crook.

As in the "Who Touched It" game, he scores 10 points if he names the right suspect. If he is wrong, everyone else gets 2 points, and the Crook 5.

How can the Detective possibly guess the right Crook purely from footprints? Easily — if he uses his eyes.

Shoes are not only of varying sizes; their soles and heels are seldom worn in the same places, and very often these differences will show up quite plainly in the prints. Sometimes, when a shoe has been newly heeled, a trademark or the name of the manufacturer will actually show up in the footprint. And some people have cleats or ridged soles on their shoes which should be easy to spot on any footprint.

In wet weather, of course, some might be wearing boots. The prints of these are very easy to distinguish from shoes — they're ridged, almost like a giant's fingerprints — and they, of course, are also liable to be worn in different places. Count the ridges, noticing which ones are faint, and you should still be able to identify the Crook even if every single suspect has turned up wearing boots! Running shoes and sneakers leave very different footprints as well.

4. THE "BLACK HAND" GAME

Now we come to the hardest of this series of games. It's so difficult that the Detective should score at least 25 points if she names the Crook. But it's such a fascinating exercise in detection that I could not resist including it.

The "Black Hand" Game is played indoors, and starts in exactly the same way as the "Who Touched It" and the "Careless Crook" games. But this time, the Crook doesn't leave fingerprints or clues. He or she is that most sinister of criminals: the anonymous threat-maker.

He or she is handed a sheet of paper, and is given *30 seconds* (not a second more) to write the following message:

BEWARE. THE BLACK HAND IS GOING TO GET YOU TONIGHT.

When the Detective comes back into the room, she has to guess the Crook's identity, using only this sample of handwriting. The Detective has five minutes to do this. She may look at the notebooks of all the members of the club or any other sample of their writing, in order to compare it with the Black Hand message. The Detective is also entitled to ask any of the suspects to write his or her name and address on a scrap of paper.

As I said, this is a hard game; but it's not quite so difficult as it sounds.

Remember, the Crook was allowed only 30 seconds to write the message; and writing ten words in 30 seconds — that's only three seconds a word — doesn't give you much chance to disguise your handwriting!

All the Detective has to do is look at the message and see if she can spot any unusual things about the writing. Everyone's handwriting, remember, is as unique as his or her fingerprints, and the peculiarities aren't too hard to spot.

Let's suppose, for example, that the handwritten message looks like this:

BEWARE!
THE BLACK HAND IS GOING TO
GET YOU TONIGHT!

You'll notice that there are some definite oddities about the way the letters are formed. The "G's" have a long downward stroke, and every time the writer makes a "T," he or she puts more of a curl into the cross stroke. It looks as though our Crook normally makes a very stylish, curly "T" and was trying to disguise it — but there were so many "T's" in that sentence that by the time the fourth one was reached the Crook was beginning to forget.

Armed with this discovery, the Detective looks at each of the suspects' notebooks, looking for peculiar "G's" and "T's." Let's say that one suspect shows him a book, on the cover of which she has written:

PAMELA WHITE 5TH GRADE
HISTORY NOTEBOOK.

One "G" with just the right downward stroke and no less than three curly "T's"!

The game is in the bag — and so are the Detective's 25 points for winning.

If the Detective names the wrong person, the Crook deserves a high score, and I suggest he or she gets 15 points. If spotting handwriting is difficult, so is disguising it — when you're writing ten words in 30 seconds flat.

5. THE "PASS ON THE FORMULA" GAME

This game works entirely differently from the others.

This time, everyone goes out of the room *except* the Crook; and the Crook isn't really a crook but a spy — a key secret service agent (emphatically in the 007 class) who has been given an extremely tough assignment. Although trapped in a room with all those enemies outside the door, he has in his possession a vitally important secret formula: "A + B = 333."

He knows that sometime soon a fellow-agent will be along this way; and it is his job to leave the formula *hidden in the room where his enemies won't spot it, but where his fellow-agent will.*

He can scrawl the formula on a piece of paper and leave it tucked between two floorboards, or screwed up in the top of a ball-point pen left casually on a desk. He can chalk it on the underside of a window-sill. He can pencil it on the inside rim of a plant pot in the corner. He can write it on a paper dart, and throw the dart so that it lands on top of a tall cupboard. He can scribble it on the outside of an empty ice-cream container and chuck it in the wastepaper basket. He can write it in the dust on the window-pane . . .

There are no limits to what our spy can do, provided that there's no damage to property, and provided that by the time the rest of the club returns to the room, the formula A + B = 333 is written, clearly and unmistakably, on something, somewhere inside the room.

This game obviously requires careful time limits. I would say that the Spy should be allowed three minutes alone in the room to hide the formula, and that the rest of the club — all of them Spy Catchers —

should be allowed three minutes in which to find it.

If they *do* find it within the required time, the finder scores 10 and everyone else 2. If they fail to find it — and the Spy can show that it has indeed been written quite clearly, under their noses all the time — then the Spy earns — and deserves — all of 25.

There are two other small rules. The Spy must not hide the formula anywhere in his clothes or on his person. And he must not hide it in anyone else's personal property, such as inside a locker or a desk. Otherwise, the game is as simple and straightforward as ABC. Or, at least, as $A + B = 333$.

By the time you've finished all these activities, you and your friends should be pretty clued-in on the subject of clues — looking for them, analyzing them, and following them up.

You are ready now to start on a more advanced kind of game: a game that involves not only fingerprinting and clue-hunting, but questioning suspects and seeing through alibis.

It's not so much a game as a full-scale opportunity for — investigation.

CHAPTER 4

Detecting for Fun— Investigating

1. THE "WHODUNIT" GAME

The more members there are in your club, the more enjoyment — and practice — you'll get out of this game.

It starts like this. You put a number of crumpled bits of paper in a hat — as many bits of paper as there are members of the club. Each piece has a word written on it. In most cases the word is *Suspect*. But one piece of paper has *Detective* written on it, and another has *Crook*.

Each member draws a piece of paper out of the hat and reads what is written on it. Then everyone except the Detective folds up his or her piece of paper, and pockets it without letting anyone else see it. The Detective spreads out his piece of paper, and shows it around.

In other words, throughout the game, everybody knows who the Detective is; but no one knows who the Crook is — except, of course, the Crook. And the

Suspects are not allowed to tell each other, or the Detective, what they are.

Now we come to the interesting part.

The Detective has to name a certain object in his possession which he challenges the Crook to steal within the next twenty-four hours.

The object must be something reasonably portable and inexpensive. (A special T-shirt, a paperback book, a small empty box — anything like that will do.) The Detective is not allowed to carry it on his person. It has to be in a reasonably accessible place — for example, his yard, bookbag, bicycle basket or garage. It should not be protected by a lock or padlock. Nor is the Detective allowed to take any special steps to guard it. If the object is kept in the Detective's desk, the Detective must not keep special watch on the desk during breaks. In other words, the Crook must have a reasonable chance.

The Crook Scores

The Crook is also restricted. He is not allowed to tell any of the Suspects who he is, or to use any of them as accomplices. And he is not allowed to wear gloves, because practice in taking fingerprints is all part of the game.

Now it could happen that the Crook is clumsy, and is caught by the Detective in the act of stealing the object. In this case, the detective scores 30 points, and the game is at an end. (Unless the Detective has set an unfair trap; in which case, the Crook gets 30 points, and again, the game is at an end.)

But if the game goes right, the Crook will succeed in making away with the object, and the Detective will *then have twenty-four hours in which to investigate the crime, find the object, and name the Crook.*

If he finds the object, he scores 25 points. If he names the Crook correctly, he scores 30 points. If he fails to find the object, the Crook scores 25 points. And if he names the wrong Suspect, the Crook scores 30 points.

(I'm afraid there's no opportunity for Suspects to win points — but after all, any of them could be Detective or Crook next time.)

Other rules are:

No Suspect can refuse to be questioned by the Detective — and they must all tell the truth. Only the Crook is allowed to lie.

The Suspects must allow the Detective to search any of their belongings at any time, and to take their fingerprints. And so, of course, must the Crook — if he doesn't want to give himself away!

The Detective is not allowed to question anyone who is not in the game, and forfeits 20 points if found doing so.

The Crook is not allowed to carry the stolen object about on his person, except immediately after the actual theft. Nor is he allowed to take the object home. It must be hidden somewhere accessible to everyone, and not in any "out-of-bounds" area.

(Again, don't select a valuable object. A real thief might come upon it accidentally, and make off with it — which *isn't* in the rules of the game!)

2. STARTING YOUR INVESTIGATION

The Detective must begin his investigation by getting out his Scene-of-the-Crime Kit (as detailed in Chapter 2); by examining the Scene of the Crime, and collecting clues.

He scores DOUBLE POINTS (60 instead of 30) if he can name the Crook on the evidence of clues alone — without questioning any of the Suspects at all.

Let's imagine that you are the Detective. Your first job is to see if you can find fingerprints.

A good way to start is by trying to decide which surfaces the Crook is most likely to have touched. If the object has been stolen from a desk, this means he probably touched the desktop. If the object has been lifted from a bicycle basket, then the Crook may well have touched the actual bike in the process of getting at the object: it would be worth powdering the handlebars and seat. And so on.

Other clues worth looking for (as you'll know if you have played the "Careless Crook" game a few times) are stray hairs, tiny bits of fabric, and any odd objects that might have dropped from the culprit's pockets, from a piece of chewing gum to a comb or pen. It's quite possible that such things *could* have been left. The Crook was probably nervous, and had to work very fast before anyone came in. Don't forget that your quarry may at some time have tried to hide — so it's worth getting out that flashlight to search for clues in the most unexpected places.

Don't forget to pick up, place in an envelope, and label every clue, as described in Chapter 3 ("The Big Clue Rule" section).

3. ALIBIS

Having examined the Scene of the Crime and collected clues (if any), the Detective goes on to question suspects and hunt for the object.

Questioning suspects is one of the most exciting things in this game.

"Where were you at two o'clock?"

Don't forget, you are in the same position as the hero in a classic detective story. You have had your list of suspects handed to you, so to speak, on a plate. You know, before you begin, that one of them *has* to be the Crook.

You simply have to keep questioning them about where they were at the time of the crime — and sooner or later, one of their alibis is bound to crack.

For example, suppose the object was stolen from your locker in the hallway at lunchtime. There are, let's say, five members of your YDC: Mike, Jane, Steve, Chris and Sandra. Jane and Sandra say that all through the lunchbreak, they were working on a science project in the science lab. Steve and Chris say that they were practicing football on the playground.

Now, remember, *Suspects* aren't allowed to lie. Jane and Sandra, Steve and Chris are thus providing alibis for each other — and since at least three out of that four must be telling the truth, it looks as if all their alibis must be okay. Therefore you can deduce straight away that Mike is liable to be the Crook.

(It isn't quite certain, though. For instance, Steve might have slipped away from the football practice without Chris noticing, or Sandra might have left the science lab saying she was going to the girl's room — without Jane remembering. A good detective never takes things for granted until he's checked!)

Once you think you know who the Crook is, don't challenge him. Keep the information to yourself — like an ace held in your hand until the end of a trick in cards — and get on to the next stage: finding the stolen object. This is a glorified game of "hunt the thimble" that could take you all over the place.

4. END OF THE "WHODUNIT" GAME

When the twenty-four hours given for the Detective's investigation are up, all the players assemble in an agreed place. In the presence of everyone, the Detective has to produce the stolen object (if he has found it) and then name the Crook.

Points are then allotted, on the scale already given, to see if the Detective or the Crook has won.

It may be that the Detective will try and score double points by naming the Crook on "Scene of the Crime" evidence alone.

In that case, each Suspect has first to testify that the Detective has not asked him or her a single question. If the Detective goes for this "Scene of the

You Dunit!

Crime" bonus, and names the wrong person, then the Crook wins the 60 bonus points instead.

Well, that's the game in a nutshell. If your club finds that any more rules are needed, then by all means go ahead and make your own. You might also experiment with shortening the time scale, or leaving out the "find-the-object" bit. You can, in fact, make any number of modifications to suit yourselves. Basically, though, I believe you will find the game intriguing and challenging. It will develop sharp eyes, sharp wits — and, in fact, sharpen every single skill you need to be a young detective.

5. THE SHERLOCK HOLMES GAME

Here is an altogether less elaborate game — but it should prove to be both challenging and fun.

Beforehand, you ask various people — obliging parents, friendly teachers, long-suffering brothers and sisters, patient friends — to lend you their briefcases, notebooks, handbags, or old coats. If the object is a briefcase or handbag, you should ask the lender not to take anything out of it, apart, of course, from money, valuables or private items. If it's a coat, he should leave the contents of the pockets untouched.

You then ask each lender to list personal details — job, home, place of work, hobbies, interests, sports, school, etc. — on a sheet of paper. You should also ask for his phone number, and make sure that it is possible to reach him during the course of the game,

Elementary, My Dear Detective

should the need arise. (There's no reason why you shouldn't have all the lenders in the audience, if they'll come.)

To start the game, you divide the club into two teams, A and B.

You pass the objects, in turn, first to one team and then the other. (Obviously, if Team A gets first look at one object, then B should have first look at the next.)

Each team then has *three minutes to deduce all it can about the owner of the object from the things which it contains.*

Someone has to act as chairman and timekeeper, and sit between the teams with a stopwatch and a gong. Someone else should also be on hand to run out to telephone the objects' owners to confirm deductions if and when required.

At the end of the three minutes, each team is allowed to make either definite statements or guesses about the object's owner. A definite statement scores 2 points if it turns out to be correct, but loses 2 points if wrong. A guess scores or loses only 1 point. Team B is obviously not allowed to repeat any of Team A's deductions, but they can turn one of Team A's guesses into a definite statement, if they have found new evidence which proves the point.

Here's an example of how the game works out.

Let's say that the first object handed to Team A is an old blue rain slicker, obviously a child's. The first thing the team must decide is whether it's a boy's slicker or a girl's. That's easy, of course; boys' coats button left over right, and girls' coats right over left. This slicker is found to be a boy's.

Next the team must look at it and try to guess the age of the boy. It seems to be about the right size for a ten- to twelve-year-old.

But wait. In the left-hand pocket of the slicker, there is a foreign coin — an English 2p piece. This could mean either:

(a) The boy has recently been to England, or

(b) Someone gave him the coin.

There are two other things in the left-hand pocket: a torn ticket to a Red Sox game and a small quantity of what looks like beach sand.

Now the price on the Red Sox ticket is 75¢. Someone says that it's been years since a ticket to a major ball game cost as little as that. No one knows how many years, but it looks as if the boy who owned the slicker is much older than ten to twelve now!

Before time runs out, somebody thinks of looking to see if there's a label inside the slicker itself. They find the name of the store at which it was bought — Macy's. This means that the boy probably lived in New York. Suddenly the team strikes gold: they find a nametag, ROGER RIVERS.

Just then the gong goes. Team A's three minutes are over. They decide that they have deduced eight things. Here they are, with the possible points gained, if the deductions prove to be correct.

1. The slicker belongs to a boy. (Definite statement: 2)

2. He was, at the time he wore it, ten to twelve years old. (Definite statement: 2)

3. He may now be sixteen to eighteen. (Guess: 1)

4. He had been on a beach. (Guess: 1)

5. He had also been to England. (Guess: 1)

6. He is a baseball fan. (Definite Statement: 2)

7. He lived in New York. (Definite statement: 2)

8. His name is Roger Rivers. (Definite statement: 2)

The slicker is now passed to Team B, who pounce on the right-hand pocket, which Team A didn't have time to empty. They find, first, a seashell — so they can turn Team A's clever guess (number 4) into a definite statement. Next, they find a New York

Yankees button. And finally they have a massive stroke of luck. They discover a tattered handbill reading:

GRAND RUMMAGE SALE
will be held at
Emmanuel Church, Boston
on behalf of
the Boy Scouts
on Sat. Feb. 10, 1973
at 3 p.m.

Now, ten- to twelve-year-old schoolboys aren't very interested in rummage sales, as a rule. The fact that Roger Rivers has a handbill for one in his pocket suggests that he was most likely distributing the bills on behalf of the Boy Scouts — which obviously means that he was a Boy Scout himself! And if he was ten to twelve in 1973, this means that Team A's guess about his present age can be increased by two years, and turned into a definite statement.

When the gong goes at the end of three minutes, Team B decides to risk five definite statements.

1. Roger Rivers was in the Boy Scouts. (2)
2. He lived in or near Boston, Massachusetts. (2)
3. He is now eighteen to twenty years old. (2)
4. He has been on vacation near a beach. (2)
5. He is a Yankee fan. (2)

At this stage, there is a short pause while Roger Rivers himself is telephoned. He confirms that both teams' statements and guesses are correct for the most part. But he is twenty years old, so Team A loses a point for their Item 3. He lives in Boston, Massachusetts, not New York, so Team A loses two points for their Item 7. He has never been to Britain (the coin was given to him by his father after a business trip) so Team A loses one point for their Item 5. And he has never been a Yankee fan. That button in his pocket must have been something he happened to pick up in the street. (Team B might have guessed that. Unless there was something wrong with the pin, a real Yankee fan would have proudly sported the badge in his lapel, not kept it in his pocket!) So Team B loses 2 points for their Item 5. Totaling up the marks, Team A scores $13 - 4 = 9$ and Team B scores $10 - 2 = 8$. Team A therefore wins this round by 1 point.

I hope that's given you some idea of how the Sherlock Holmes Game is played. For some practice in making deductions, and further hints, please turn to the next chapter.

CHAPTER 5

Making Deductions

1. THE FACE AT THE WINDOW

One late October night, at about nine o'clock, I was sitting at a table in my dining room, writing. My wife had a cold, and had gone to bed early. The children had gone out somewhere for the evening. I was all by myself on the ground floor of the house.

Across the room, straight in front of me on the other side of the table, was a pair of french windows. I hadn't bothered to draw the curtains, and through the windows could just be glimpsed a moonlit garden. It was a fairly windy night. Every so often, I could hear a creaking sound, which I took to be the branches of a rosebush brushing against the top of the garden fence, just to the right of the french windows. The only other sound was a faint beat of rock music, being played somewhere in the house next door. It was presumably being played by the boy who lived there — rock music being his big joy in life, apart from football and hockey.

Well, there I was, sitting in the dining room writing, when suddenly I heard something — or someone — tapping against the window. I looked up — and started violently. Just outside the window, a hideous bright green face was staring at me. I couldn't see any sign of a body being attached to it. There was just this green face, surrounded by darkness.

Suddenly it started swaying from side to side. Then it began to rise and fall. One minute it was near the top of the window; the next it was halfway down, almost level with the latch; the next, it was back near the top again.

By this time, I was on my feet. I wasn't shaking with terror. I was chuckling, and heading for the kitchen — in search of a pair of scissors, and a flashlight.

Can you deduce why?

The answer isn't very difficult, if you followed the clues I hid in the story. It was a late October night — in other words, round about Halloween, the time when kids are apt to play tricks. Just to the right of the french windows was a garden fence, which had been creaking. And the interests of the boy next door included hockey.

It wasn't hard for me to work out:

1. That the face was in reality a Halloween mask (a lot are in the shops around the end of October).

2. That it must be dangling from something (or it wouldn't swing from side to side).

3. That the "something" must itself be movable

(otherwise the mask couldn't rise and fall three feet in a second).

4. That it was, in all probability, a hockey stick, stuck over the top of the fence from next door. (The boy's first attempts to push the stick over the fence had probably caused the creaking.)

I went to the kitchen to get a pair of scissors in the hope of being able to run out of the back door, rush around outside the french windows, and cut the string on which the mask was dangling. But in fact, by the time I got out there, there was nothing to be seen.

There was something to be heard, though.

Some choice language came floating across from the other side of the fence.

"Blast, I've got my —— caught on a rusty nail."

I didn't quite catch what.

But I had heard enough to know that my conclusions were correct. And that the habit of deduction had saved me from getting quite a fright.

2. THE TWELVE-FOOT FOOTBALL FAN

We all of us make deductions, of some kind or other, every day of our lives.

When we're lying in bed early on a Sunday morning, and are awakened by a thump from the direction of the hall, we turn over and go to sleep again — because we've deduced that it's only the Sunday paper being delivered on the front porch.

When an electric bulb fails to light up after we've clicked on the switch, we deduce that the lamp is unplugged or there's been a power failure. On the other hand, if there's a flash before the light goes out, we deduce that the bulb has blown. And so on.

But the *habit* of deduction — which really means drawing conclusions from things that an ordinary person wouldn't even notice — is definitely the sign of a young detective.

Let's suppose you're sitting in the waiting room at a train station. The train you're waiting for is very late, and you're getting very bored.

Suddenly you find yourself staring at something written high up on one of the walls, only a couple of inches below where the ceiling begins. The writing puzzles you, because every fourth letter tails away in a descending squiggle.

FIGHT-DALLAS COWBOYS!

The words are obviously a football fan's message. But why is every fourth letter written so oddly? You wonder if it's meant to be some kind of code.

And while you're wondering that, something else strikes you.

How could the words have come to be written at all?

You judge that they are a good twelve feet from the ground. Most people write on walls at eye-level. That is, someone who's six feet tall would write at a height of about five feet eight inches. To go any higher, he'd have to be writing above his head, an awkward process that rapidly produces arm-ache. But even a giant of seven feet, stretching his arms to their fullest extent, couldn't write at twelve feet above the floor.

Unless, of course, he stood on something . . .

With curiosity now thoroughly aroused, you look around the waiting room. There is only one seat, and that is fixed to the floor. There is a table, but that is nailed down, too. And neither the seat nor the table — nor any of the windowsills — are anywhere near the wall with the mysterious writing. There isn't any radiator or pipe anywhere near it, either.

Baffled, you stare dazedly up at the words . . . and the puzzling squiggled letters . . . and suddenly everything clicks into place, and you know just how they were written.

Don't you?

The answer, like most deductions, is really only a matter of common sense.

If the writer wasn't standing on some*thing*, he must have been standing on some*body!*

In other words, he must have asked a friend to bend over, while he stood on his back. Probably, they were both half drunk. Certainly, neither of them were steady on their legs — because every few seconds, the friend started wobbling and the writer made those strange squiggly letters — exactly the letters that would have been made by somebody falling, or about to fall! The letters occur regularly because presumably, after each jump-up, the friend managed to keep steady for the same microscopic length of time.

Now here's a problem that you ought to be able to solve in five seconds flat.

Supposing you've found a wallet in the street — or have been handed one as part of a Sherlock Holmes game. Inside the wallet are two envelopes, both containing letters. Envelope number 1 has a stamp; is postmarked Denver, Colorado; and has been slit open at the top. It is addressed to: Simon Grafton, 13 Sunnyvale Gardens, San Francisco, California. Envelope number 2 also has a stamp, but it is not postmarked and has not been opened. It is addressed to: Mrs. C. Fairlie, 37 Walton Street, Denver, Colorado. Who would you deduce to be the owner of the wallet?

The answer must be Mr. Simon Grafton.

The Final Analysis

People only carry two kinds of letters in their wallets, as a general rule: (1) letters which they have received in the mail and want to read again; or (2) letters which they have just written, but haven't mailed yet.

Since envelope number 2 didn't carry a postmark but does have a stamp, it was obviously destined for the mailbox. And must have been written *by*, not *to*, the wallet's owner.

There's another way you could have guessed at the answer — and that would have taken only one second. You could think that it had to be Simon Grafton — because whoever heard of a woman carrying a wallet? But then you might find yourself surprised by how many do. Don't let yourself take things for granted when you're deducing. Test every theory.

4. THE DETECTIVE'S FRIENDS

Letters, Licenses. Lists. And tickets.

Whether you find them in a wallet, handbag, or coat, these are the four greatest aids to deducing facts about the owner.

Letters are invaluable because, in practice, you will find that 90 percent of the letters people carry around are addressed to themselves. The others — the about-to-be-mailed ones — are easy to spot, as we've seen.

A Driver's License tells you the owner's name and address for certain.

A List — especially a shopping list — can often tell you a great deal about the person who wrote it. From the quantities of food mentioned, you can make a reasonable guess at the size or his or her family or the size of his or her appetite! (Although people don't usually buy three pounds of sausages or twenty fish sticks if they're living alone.) If the list includes stockings or perfume, you're obviously more likely to be dealing with a woman than a man. If you see Heinz or Gerber's Baby Foods, it's probably a mother's list. Whereas a list that includes hefty do-it-yourself stuff (say, taking a Black & Decker power drill in for repair) would more likely indicate a man. But not certainly. Work on that basis, but don't be surprised if it's wrong. Incidentally, there is no way of telling a woman's handwriting from a man's. Not even the world's greatest handwriting experts can do this — so how can anyone else hope to?

Tickets, receipts, or charge cards no matter how torn or battered, are always worth looking at very carefully. A library card carries the owner's full name and address, and so is as good as finding an identity card! A season ticket (bus or rail) almost always means that the owner works — or, in the case of a child, attends school — at or near the place mentioned on the ticket. Monthly railway tickets carry the owner's name, although this can be scrawled unreadably. A bus ticket always gives the number of the bus, the date, the place of departure and the destination — but you'd have to know the route very well to be able to decipher it at a glance. Other tickets — for movies, theaters, concerts, racetracks, football or baseball stadiums, bingo halls, discos, skating rinks, bowling

For Future Reference

alleys, whatever — can speak volumes about the person's hobbies and way of life.

5. A CLUES SCRAPBOOK

Unfortunately, tickets don't always state clearly what they are. A movie ticket can look very like one for a baseball game — to someone who doesn't regularly go to the movies or ballgames.

It's not a bad idea to start collecting tickets issued by the train and bus companies, cinemas, theaters and other show-places in your area. You might paste them into a special "Clues Scrapbook," and keep looking at them until you can identify each ticket on sight.

It'd be a great moment if you could take one glance at the contents of a wallet, and announce airily:

"Ah, yes. This belongs to a Mrs. Joanna West. She lives at 14 Ash Street, Norwell; has at least two children, one of them a baby; goes to work in Belmont every day; likes to go to the movies and play bingo, and last Saturday, she took a bus to West Kingsley, getting on at the stop before High Street."

A staggering series of deductions — but a single envelope, a short shopping-list, and just four tickets could give you the clues to them all.

CHAPTER 6

Secret Messages

1. CONCEALING MESSAGES IN LETTERS

See if you can deduce what's odd about this letter.

> 73 Chestnut Street
> Boston,
> Massachusetts 0210<u>6</u>

Dear Jill,

I was very pleased to see you yesterday. But I bet you are like me today — feeling under the weather after Aunt Lizzie's cherry wine!

I know I drank tree glasses. I'm sure you had at least as many. Perhaps even four!

Hope we're both okay by Wednesday.

> Love, Sandra.

If you've sharp eyes, you'll spot at once that there's something strange about the postal code after the address. Numbers in postal codes never have to be underlined — so what's that little line doing under that 6? Then, again, judging from the rest of the letter, Sandra is a pretty good speller. So why should she have left out the "h" in "three"?

It looks as if this letter contains a secret message, and that the key to it is the number 6. So let's see what happens if we take every sixth word.

Dear Jill,

I was very pleased to SEE you yesterday. But I bet YOU are like me today — feeling UNDER the weather after Aunt Lizzie's CHERRY wine!

I know I drank TREE glasses. I'm sure you had AT least as many. Perhaps even FOUR!

Hope we're both okay by WEDNESDAY.

Love, Sandra.

Pretty clear now, isn't it? Sandra is telling Jill that she wants to see her under the cherry tree at four o'clock on Wednesday. Under this system, you can use every second, third, fourth, fifth, sixth or even sixtieth word! It's entirely up to you, so long as you hide the number somewhere in the letter as a key. The chief snag with the method is that it's terribly hard to make your letter sound natural, particularly when awkward words like "cherry" have to be worked in. Since Sandra's message was such a short one, she'd have done better to have written it on the envelope, in very small print, and covered it up with a stamp. She could have put LUS (LOOK UNDER STAMP) as a PS to signal to Jill what she was doing.

Incidentally, to be sure of being able to read a message written under a stamp, you shouldn't pull the stamp off too roughly. Ideally, you should take the envelope into the kitchen, and hold the stamp part over a steaming kettle for a couple of minutes. Then the stamp will peel easily away, leaving the words underneath intact. But watch out that you don't get your fingers too close to the steam!

Private Eyes?

2. INVISIBLE INK

A third method of concealing a message in a letter is with invisible writing. It may surprise you to know that you already have a bottle of invisible ink in your house. In fact you probably have two or three quarts of it. You'll find it in the kitchen, in the refrigerator — and it usually goes under the name of milk.

Pour a little milk into a jar or glass. Into this, dip a small paint brush, or the quill end of a large feather, or a pen holder with a plain nib in it — anything will do as long as you can write with it, and not make a visible mark.

You will find there is one difficulty about writing in milk. The stuff takes a long time — over an hour — to dry, and if you blot it, it spoils the invisible message. You have to be pretty patient; but it really is worth it. If you end a letter with a message written in milk, it really is totally invisible. Even if you hold the letter up to the light, or look at it through a magnifying glass, you will find it impossible to make out a single word, and usually, there is absolutely no sign that there is a message there at all.

Yet hold the letter close to a fire, or against a hot radiator, and every word will come up in bright browny-yellow letters, crisp and clear.

Some people prefer to use vinegar, which doesn't take so long to dry. But make sure you use *white* vinegar. With the brown kind, the message is never really invisible. Secret agents traditionally use lemon juice, which certainly works quite well, but is a bit sticky on the pen.

3. WATCH OUT — EAVESDROPPERS!

There are occasions when you may want to send a secret message by voice.

Let's suppose you're having a private telephone conversation with a friend, and you want to tell him: "Watch out. Someone has just come into the room, and I can't speak freely."

The best thing is to be prepared beforehand for such a situation. Have a code phrase ready, so that whenever you use it, your friend will know that your conversation is being listened to.

How about *"Speak louder — I can't hear you"*? That can be used in most telephone conversations, and won't raise any suspicions.

4. SECRET MESSAGES BY PHONE

But it may not be enough to be able to warn a friend against eavesdroppers. There may be occasions when you want to send a full message, when there are people about who are bound to overhear. The only answer to this is to have a whole list of code phrases, which you and your friends learn by heart.

I can't give you a full list, because I've no idea what sort of message you might want to send. But here's a tip. Don't choose unusual or outlandish phrases. It's much better to use those silly little words that people say all the time without realizing it — "well," "uh-huh," "you know," "er," "yes," "m'm," and "okay?" Nobody pays any attention when they hear words like these, because they are quite meaningless — noises made by people who can't sort out quickly enough what they really want to say. If you turn these words into code-phrases, you can slip quite complicated messages into a conversation without anybody else noticing what's happening at all.

Here are a few examples. They look pretty silly written down, and they'll sound pretty silly when you

The Lurking Listener

first use them. But after a bit of practice, I think you'll find that they'll work very well. And if you and your friends develop a full code, using these "er" words as building bricks, you'll soon be able to pass secret messages to each other as easily as whistling a tune.

PHRASE	MEANING
Cough, followed by "Sorry about that."	Watch out. I'll be using code phrases from now on.
A "you know" during a sentence, followed by "okay?" at the end. (*Example: "I'm not, you know, into punk rock yet, okay?"*)	The gang is holding an emergency meeting tonight.
M'm . . . yes . . .	At the usual place.
Uh-huh . . .	At the usual time.
Yeah . . . well . .	Make sure you let everybody know.
Okay? Okay? (Twice)	What's the new password?
You'll . . . er . . . (*Example: "You'll . . . er . . . be hearing from me tomorrow"*)	I've written you a letter. Watch for message under stamp.
Well, then . . . (*Example: "Well, then, I'll be seeing you sometime"*)	I've written you a letter. Watch for PS in invisible ink.
Cough, followed by "Sorry, sorry"	No more messages. Rest of conversation normal.

5. ANNOUNCING SECRET MEETINGS

If you're in a secret society at school, it often becomes necessary to hold meetings at short notice — and the problem is to let everybody know about them without giving away the fact that you *are* all in a secret society.

Let's suppose that two of your members are standing, talking, in a group of children who know nothing about the society. And suppose you want to let your members know about the meeting without arousing any outsider's suspicions about what is going on. Once again, a prearranged code phrase is the answer.

You walk up to the group and say: "Can anyone tell me the time? My watch has gone haywire. It says 4:15." 4:15 is, of course, the time of the meeting. None of the outsiders in the group will dream that you've passed on a secret announcement. They will all be too busy looking at their own watches, ready to tell you the right time!

Special Delivery

Another good way to call a secret meeting is to put an invisible notice on the school board.

This isn't half as difficult as it sounds. Most notice-boards tend to have odd thumbtacks sticking into them, where old notices have been taken down and people haven't bothered to remove the pins. All you have to do is stick a few thumbtacks of your own on the board, forming a special pattern. Your members will recognize it straight away, and will know they are being called to a meeting. No one else will notice anything odd about the board at all. You can even use the tacks to state precisely when and where the meeting's being held. For example, five pins in a "U" pattern would mean: "Usual place at five."

6. MESSAGES IN MORSE

I don't suppose you need me to tell you how many ways there are of sending secret written messages around at school. You can conceal a slip of paper in the top of a ball-point pen: slice an eraser in two halves, then stick it together with a message hidden in the middle; wedge a bit of paper under the inside front flap of a book jacket, and so on.

But all that is kid's stuff. The really clever operators are the ones who can tap out a message on a radiator so that it can be picked up five rooms down the corridor — or who can knock on a bedroom wall and pass the results of a football match on to the boy next door.

Cracking the Code

To do this, you have to know the Morse Code by heart — which is something very, very few people do.

I'm not sure why, because the whole thing only takes a couple of hours to learn, and after a few evenings' practice at sending Morse messages, you'll never forget a letter of it for as long as you live.

Here it is:

A .–	J .–––	S ...
B –...	K –.–	T –
C –.–.	L .–..	U ..–
D –..	M ––	V ...–
E .	N –.	W .––
F ..–.	O –––	X –..–
G ––.	P .––.	Y –.––
H	Q ––.–	Z ––..
I ..	R .–.	

This code has been the standby of secret agents ever since it was invented in 1832. It has been tapped on the walls of innumerable prison cells. Lights have flashed it up to planes; whistles and foghorns have blasted it across the seas; it has even been sent by waving flags. During the Second World War, as I expect you know, one letter of it, the famous Victory V (dot dot dot dash) was drummed endlessly over the air by the BBC in England to encourage the Resistance movements in Europe. And the Morse S O S signal (dot dot dot dash dash dash dot dot dot), sent by wireless telegraphers on ships and planes, has saved more lives than anyone can begin to count.

Dots, don't forget, are tapped rapidly, and dashes more slowly, with a single (very slight) pause between letters. To avoid confusion at the other end, I'd advise you to leave a full second between every word. If you're signalling by flashlight, lantern, or the headlights of a car, then obviously you use short and long flashes, with the same pauses between letters and words.

To end this chapter where we began, Morse dots and dashes can also be used to include a hidden message in a letter. Several well-known spies used to do this by making almost imperceptible pinpricks between the lines, but I don't recommend you try this method. It's very hard on the fingers of the sender and the eyes of the receiver.

But there's no reason why you shouldn't conceal a bit of Morse in a drawing.

You remember Sandra's every-sixth-word "secret message" letter, asking Jill to meet her at four o'clock under a cherry tree on Wednesday? Let's suppose that Jill writes a reply to it, and ends her note like this:

lots of luck

Jill

This says "OK CU AT FOUR" so simply and neatly that I think it deserves a prize. But probably not a bottle of Aunt Lizzie's cherry wine.

CHAPTER 7

Codes and Code-Breaking

1. MAKING UP YOUR OWN CODE

The safest secret messages are the ones sent in code — not the Morse code (which anyone can look up if they want to) but a special code, known only to the sender of the message and his or her friends.

It's really quite simple to make up a code of your own.

First, you get a sheet of graph paper. Then you write down the alphabet, putting each letter in a separate square.

A B C D E F G H I J K L M N O P Q R S T U V W X Y Z

Now you write down a second alphabet underneath the first. But not *exactly* underneath it. You move your second alphabet two, three or four squares along to the left. (Eight, nine or ten squares, if you like. It's the positioning of the second alphabet against the first that gives you the code and since this is your code, that's entirely up to you.) Let's say you choose to make it four squares. Then you'd get:

A B C D E F G H I J K L M N O P Q R S T U V W X Y Z
A B C D E F G H I J K L M N O P Q R S T U V W X Y Z A B C

Notice, by the way, that after Z, on the second row, you start the alphabet again.

Congratulations. You have now got your own personal, private code. Copy it out a few times, and hand it to all the friends to whom you may want to send messages.

With this diagram in front of you, it only takes a minute to put any sentence into code. You simply swap each letter for its "code" letter in the square below.

Instead of A, you write D. Instead of B, you write E. Instead of K, you write N. And so on, all the way to Z (which now becomes C)!

Supposing you wanted to write: THE PASSWORD IS NOW "BLACK CAT." The coded message would read: WKH SDVVZRUG LV QRZ "EODFN FDW." Simple, isn't it?

And don't forget, if by any chance your code should fall into enemy hands, you can make yourself a new one straight away — simply by redrawing the two alphabets, and moving the bottom one a few more squares to the left.

2. MORE COMPLICATED CODES

There are plenty of more complicated codes you can use. For example, you can write your second alphabet back to front, starting with Z and ending with A. (In this case there's no need to move it a few squares along — although there's no law against doing so, if you want to.)

Another method is to put numbers in the bottom row instead of letters — but this isn't too satisfactory, because the numbers soon get into two figures, which can be confusing.

A more spectacular system is to make up your own alphabet, using a little drawing to represent every letter. (An apple for A, perhaps, a daisy for D, a cat for C and so on.) But unless you keep the drawings very simple, you're going to find writing long messages very tiring. Another method (once used by a villain in a Sherlock Holmes story) is to draw stick men — running for A, jumping for B, lying down for C, and so on.

It doesn't really matter what you do — as long as you end up with a clear and unmistakable symbol for every letter of the alphabet. And as long as you don't forget to let your friends know which code you are using, and make sure they have the key.

3. SOME SECRETS OF CODE-BREAKING

As a young detective, you aren't only interested in *making* codes. You might well have to try your hand at solving one.

At first sight, this seems a completely impossible thing to do. Imagine yourself suddenly coming across a message like this:

UIF LFZ UP UIF HBSBHF EPPS JT JO UIF TIFE

How, you wonder, could anyone begin to solve it?

The answer is, by a combination of patience, guess-work, common sense — and knowing a few basic facts about the English language.

The first rule of code-breaking is a very *eeeeeasy* one to remember. "E" occurs more often than any other letter in the alphabet. So you count up how many times each letter occurs in the coded message, and the one that turns up most often is likely to be an "E." If it isn't an "E," it's probably a "T," which is the second most common letter.

Message in the Window

In the message above, "F" occurs most often. It turns up, in fact, no less than six times, so it's a fair guess that it stands for "E."

Writing all the other letters as dots, this gives us:

.. E .E . ... .. E .... E ... . E .. E

That doesn't seem to have helped much. But now let's see what's the second most frequently used letter in the message. We find that it's "U," which occurs four times. So let's take another chance — and assume that all the "U"s stand for "T"s.

T.E . E . T.T.E .... E ... . T.E
.. E .

Let's look at the whole sentence again. You'll notice that the word T.E occurs three times. It must be a word that's used very often indeed. What's the most-used word in almost any sentence? Obviously "THE." So let's turn all the "T.E"s into "THE"s. To do this, we have to assume that "I" stands for "H." And so, to be logical, we must change that "I" in the last word into "H" too.

Now we've got:

THE .E. T. THE .... E ... . THE .. E.

The next step is to concentrate on that two-letter word, "T.". Two-letter words are easy to decode, once you know one of the two letters. If it's a consonant, you know that the other letter has to be a vowel. If it's a vowel, you know the other letter has to be a consonant. So the . in that "T." word has to be "A," "E," "I," "O," "U," or "Y." And it can't be "E," because we already know that in this code, "F" stands for "E."

So the word must be "TA," "TI," "TO," "TU," or "TY" — and obviously, it's "TO." This means that throughout the sentence, "P" must stand for "O."

This gives us:

THE.E.TO THE . . . . . E.OO. . . . . THE .HE.

Now that we've decoded so many letters, it's time to think about the code itself. We know that "F" becomes "E," "U" becomes "T," "I" becomes "H," and "P" becomes "O." On that basis, we can probably work out the enemy's whole code system. Write out the two alphabets you used in code making, and arrange the second line so that "F" comes under "E," "U" under "T," and so on.

A B C D E F G H I J K L M N O P Q R S T U V W X Y Z
A B C D E F G H I J K L M N O P Q R S T U V W X Y Z A

Not a very difficult code, as it turns out. The second alphabet was only moved one square to the left! Now, using this diagram, it's simple to translate the whole message:

THE KEY TO THE GARAGE DOOR IS IN THE SHED

4. THE CODE-BREAKER'S CODE

Here is a list of the most important things to remember in code-breaking. You could call it the Code-breaker's Code.

1. Always start by counting up the number of times each letter occurs in the coded message.

2. "E" is the most frequently occurring letter, "T" the next. After these come "A," "O," "N," "I," "R," and "S" — all six of them about equal in frequency.

3. One of the letters in any 2-letter word has to be "A," "E," "I," "O," "U," or "Y."

4. More than half the words in the language end in "E," "S," "D," or "T."

5. More than half begin with "T," "A," "O," "S," or "W."

6. A letter forming a word on its own is certain to be "A" or "I" — unless it's the initial of someone's name.

7. A word ending in "G" is very likely to end "ING."

8. The most common three-letter words are "THE" and "AND."

And don't forget, of course, to do your alphabet diagrams as soon as you've decoded enough letters to make it worthwhile.

5. TRY YOUR HAND

Finally, here are three code messages for you to take a crack at yourself.

The first two shouldn't prove too difficult. The third is just a little harder. You'll find the answers at the foot of page 88.

1: WKH HQHPB LV RQ WKH WUDLQ.
2: OGGV AQW WPFGT VJG EJGTTA VTGG.
3: SVOK NV. R ZN YVRMT ZGGZXPVW.

CHAPTER 8

Disguises

1. DETECTIVES IN DISGUISE

In a sense, a detective is always in disguise. The very word "detective" means a special kind of policeman —a policeman in plain clothes. And why is he in plain clothes? To disguise what he is from the criminals he's chasing!

Policemen in the Criminal Investigation Department—the plainclothes branch of a police force— normally try to dress as simply as possible. The last thing they want to do is stand out from the crowd. But of course, when they are in a special crowd—a crowd of baseball fans, for example—they *will* stand out unless they dress as casually and colorfully as the others.

Similarly, FBI men often dress up as toughs when they are going to raid a house in a tough district.

But the time when a detective really goes in for disguise is when he takes on what is called an "under-cover" assignment. "Undercover" work means that you spend weeks, or even months, pretending to be somebody else — usually so that you can keep close watch on a No. 1 suspect.

Let's say that Superintendent Hanley of the New York police suspects that the manager of a big jeweler's store on the Upper East Side is the mastermind behind a gang of thieves. One day, he learns that the jeweler's shop is advertising for staff. So he sends his assistant, Detective Sergeant Drake, along to the store to apply for a job. Working at the jeweler's day by day, Drake should be perfectly placed to get evidence against the suspected manager.

Now it would be no use for Drake to apply for that job looking and sounding like a detective sergeant. He has to try and turn himself into a completely different person. Let's say he decides to call himself Mr. Harold Quill. Probably he will use a few stage tricks — donning a pair of spectacles, for instance, or rubbing talcum powder into his hair every morning to make it look grayer — but he won't use anything too elaborate. Wigs and false noses get very annoying when you have to wear them day after day!

But it isn't enough for Drake just to say that he is Mr. Harold Quill, and make a few minor changes in his appearance. If he wants his undercover assignment to be a success, he will have to decide exactly what sort of person Harold Quill is — his age, his

Answers to code teasers in the last chapter:
1. THE ENEMY IS ON THE TRAIN.
2. MEET YOU UNDER THE CHERRY TREE.
3. HELP ME. I AM BEING ATTACKED.

clothes, his habits, what newspaper he reads, what food he likes, what TV programs he watches, how he walks, how he talks, how he thinks. And he will have to *live the part* for every moment of every day — or at least, every working day when he is at the jeweler's.

In other words — to be a detective on an under-cover assignment, you can't just put on a false mustache and a funny nose. You have to invent, and then become, an entirely different *you*.

Incognito

2. A DISGUISE PARTY

Back in Chapter 4 *(Detecting for Fun)* I suggested that your Detective Club might like to hold a Disguise Party. This would be nothing like a costume party. A costume party is normally intended to raise laughs — and the more outlandish the costume and makeup, the better. A Detectives' Disguise Party is, on the other hand, a serious contest to see which boy or girl can assume, for the evening, a personality most unlike their own.

A Change of Face

3. INVENTING ANOTHER *YOU*

The first thing you have to do is think up a character to play. Let's suppose you are a thin, sports-loving boy. A good character for you to choose would be a fat, book-loving one.

You start by making up a name for him — say, Peter Peabody. Now you have to set about bringing him to life in your mind. You have to decide where he lives; what school he goes to; what books he likes, and so on.

Then you try to imagine:

1. What he would wear. A fat, bookish boy might well wear corduroy pants and a button-down shirt and V-necked sweater. He might well wear glasses. Of course, a lot depends on what you can borrow. Don't forget to borrow clothes a couple of sizes too large. You're going to have to "fatten up" for the part — I suggest you put two throw pillows under your belt, side by side. The sweater will hide them nicely.

2. The way he would walk. As a fat person, he'd probably take shorter steps, and possibly faster ones. Practice this for half an hour or so.

3. The way he would stand. He'd probably stand rather primly, with his hands behind his back or his arms folded in front of him.

4. The way he would sit. Let's say he always crosses his legs, but rather awkwardly, with his left foot ending up just above his right knee (or the other way around).

5. The way he would talk. This is the most important part. The success of your whole characterization will depend on how successfully you can change your way of speaking. Don't try anything too unnatural — you'll never be able to keep it up for the whole evening! I imagine Peter Peabody talking in a rather high-pitched voice, but slowly and precisely, pronouncing each word very, very carefully. You need to practice this for two hours at least.

Have you begun to get the idea? Whatever character you dream up, you've got to try and become him — and if you can visualize the way he dresses, walks, stands, sits, and talks, you're already well on the way to achieving a disguise that is more than skin deep.

Let's go through that checklist again — this time for the girls.

Let's say you're a rather shy, sensitive girl. A good character for you to play would be a way-out rock fan. First of all, give her a name — say, Fiona Fairfax. Now go through the basics — deciding where she lives, what school she goes to, etc. If she's a rock fan, it's important to think what albums and groups she'd rave over. Now consider:

1. What she would wear. I've got to be careful here. Fashions change so fast that whatever I suggest, it's liable to be old-hat before this book is in print. Probably the best thing is to get along to a local club and take notes. But at a guess, I'd say that a T-shirt, with some outlandish message on it, and a battered pair of jeans would very probably be okay. Don't forget earrings, scarves, belts, bracelets and things like that.

2. How she would walk. Slowly, casually, unless there's some music in the background, in which case she'd probably move in time to it.

3. How she would stand. Probably she wouldn't stand. She'd lean up against things, hands in pockets.

4. How she would sit. Never stiffly. She'd always lean back, as if she owned the chair.

5. How she would talk. Again I have to be careful. Pop jargon changes as fast as pop fashion, and just as unpredictably. But I imagine she'd put in a lot of "you know"s and say "okay?" at the end of every other sentence. And she'd speak in a "take it or leave it" way, in a bored drawl.

Please remember — I'm not for a moment suggesting that you play these actual characters. I'm just showing you how you should *think a character through*.

4. ALTERING YOUR APPEARANCE

If you are dressed completely differently, and talking, walking, sitting, and standing in a different way, you have already changed your appearance quite considerably. The rest of the disguise need only consist of one or two subtle touches — unless you're being extremely ambitious, and deciding to come as Jamaican, Japanese, or Indian, when you're not.

In such cases, you'd have to use stage makeup, obtainable from your nearest theatrical costumers, whose address you'll find in the Yellow Pages. Just to be helpful, I've consulted a book on stage makeup, and I can tell you that to blacken your skin, a good

A True Test

preparation is Max Factor Pancake Negro No. 2, applied with a sponge dampened with Max Factor No. 273 Body Tint; to look Chinese or Japanese, you need Max Factor 24 Pancake (for girls) or 26 Pancake (for boys); and to look like an Indian, you need Max Factor Indian Pancake or Panstick. Ask the shop for more detailed advice on what to buy and how to apply it. The same goes for all black readers who wish to appear white.

But except for such special instances, I wouldn't advise using stage makeup at all. Stage makeup is designed to be worn in a theater, under bright lights with the audience some distance from you; it looks appallingly phony when used as part of a detective's disguise.

How can you change your appearance, then?

A lot depends, of course, on the character you want to play. A change from being thin to being fat can, as I've already suggested, be accomplished by a couple of throw pillows. A pair of glasses, if you can manage to borrow some, can be a great help; but looking through someone else's glasses that have a prescription for even a few minutes can give you a blinding headache, but many sunglasses are only slightly tinted and often look like regular glasses.

One thing you should certainly do is alter your hairstyle. If you're a girl, you're lucky; you can give your hair an entirely new look just by experimenting in front of a mirror. If you're a boy, there isn't too much you can do — except by parting your hair differently and making it look wildly untidy if it is normally smooth, or smooth if it's normally wild. There are a lot of hair creams (such as Brylcream) available at most drugstores which will help the smoothing process. Two minutes with a hairbrush (brushing it the wrong way) will make it as untidy as any absent-minded professor's. Most department stores carry wigs, but they can be expensive. Other tricks you can use are:

Making your ears stand out by wedging pieces of plasticine behind them. (Most toy stores carry plasticine.)

Making your eyebrows look sharper or bushier with an eyebrow pencil — found at any drugstore or department store in the cosmetic section.

Making yourself look older by running an eyebrow pencil along the wrinkles in your forehead, and also along the lines between your nostrils and your mouth. (If you haven't got even the faintest wrinkles or lines in those places, forget it!)

5. JUDGING THE DISGUISES

Judging a Young Detectives' Disguise Party is rather a different matter from judging a costume party.

Marks have to be given for how well each contestant has thought out the character he is portraying, as well as how skillfully he has actually changed his voice and his appearance.

I suggest that the judges should sit behind a table, and cross-examine each contestant for about three minutes. If the contestant can answer questions about his or her likes, dislikes, imaginary parents, home, school and so on without getting caught out — *and* without slipping back to his or her natural voice — then obviously very high points are scored.

The judges, of course, ought to be people who know the contestants pretty well. Otherwise how can they tell how cleverly they're disguised? Ideally, they should be fellow-members of the club, whose names have been taken out of a hat. If they don't like the idea of being judges, and are afraid you'll all grumble at their decisions, simply smile sweetly.

And suggest that *they* come in disguise.

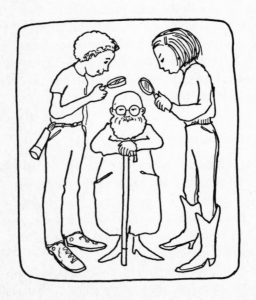

Who is This?

CHAPTER 9

Clever Stuff

1. TAPE RECORDERS

This chapter is intended for what you might call the more advanced students.

Up to now, this book has only mentioned simple and cheap detective equipment. But for older readers, or readers lucky enough to have a big allowance or have friends who might own the equipment, here are some more expensive items that would be worth using.

A tape recorder, for example, is a very useful aid when you are questioning suspects in the "Whodunit" game. You can listen to each person's story again and again — and recapture not only the facts, but exactly the way they were told to you.

There is another big advantage to a tape-recorded interview. It prevents arguments about what a person actually said.

2. CAMERAS

As that seventeen-year-old girl discovered back in Chapter 1, a movie camera is just about the handiest device ever invented for crime-spotting!

For a Scene-of-the-Crime Kit, the most valuable addition would be a color or black-and-white Polaroid camera, with a flash attachment for indoor shots. (With a Polaroid, you can develop any picture in a few seconds, on the spot.)

The clues that it would be most useful to photograph are things like footprints and tire tracks, which can be extremely awkward sometimes to draw or trace.

It can also be useful to have an overall shot of the whole Scene of the Crime.

3. THE LAST LAUGH

Incidentally, if you happen to live near a high-quality joke shop, and you still have some money to spare, I would recommend buying one of those electronic boxes or bags that give out peal after peal of ghostly laughter when they are touched.

' The next time you suspect that someone is snooping about in your desk or locker, or going through the pockets of coats in the locker room, just leave the laugh box in a desk, locker or pocket at the scene of his suspected activities.

You needn't stay too close yourself. Once the box is triggered off, the peals of laughter should be heard across the entire school building. And it won't hurt to give the snoop a chance to get clear. He's unlikely ever to venture near anyone else's private property again.

On the Spot

4. MODERN DETECTION EQUIPMENT

Now, just to make you green with envy, here are some of the multi-thousand-dollar devices available to today's police detectives.

1. A videotape camera, with sound-recording gear — exactly like the ones used to film TV newsreel shots — can now be taken to the scene of a major crime. It can be used to film moving clues — for example, the way a door opens or shuts; or to capture sounds, such as the kind of creak made when a particular stair is trodden on. The police sometimes attempt to reconstruct a crime in front of the camera, with detectives playing the parts of criminal and victim. Running the scene through over and over again can often give new clues to exactly how the crime was committed.

For example, let's imagine a murder case in which the victim was struck from behind while he was sitting in an armchair reading a book. The blow landed on the back of his head, so it is obvious that he didn't turn around when his murderer entered the room. The police set up videotape equipment with sound-recording gear and film the scene in the room where it happened, with one detective playing the murderer and another the victim. They run the film through half a dozen times, and suddenly a very significant fact strikes them. The door of the room creaks as it opens, a slight sound, but loud enough for anyone sitting in the armchair to hear. In other words, the victim must have heard the murderer enter, but didn't bother to turn his head to see who it was. Why? Obviously, it must have been someone he knew very well, and who was always coming in and out of the room — in other words, his wife or some other member of the family! A vital clue, but it might easily have been missed if the police hadn't reenacted the crime on the spot and watched the result again and again.

2. *A laser-beam detector device* has recently been invented which can measure the slightest dent made when anyone walks across a carpet. This is a very important discovery, because in these days of wall-to-wall

The Electronic Detective

carpeting, it is rare for any indoor crime to be committed without the crook, at some stage, walking across a carpet. This laser-beam detector actually makes a "holograph" (that is, a three-dimensional image) of the dent, from which the detectives can make a shrewd guess as to the height, weight and build of the criminal. All — remember — from a dent so slight that it would be quite invisible to the naked eye!

3. *A spectrometer* has now been developed which can analyze the most microscopic fragment of paint or glass found sticking to anyone's clothing, with quite staggering results. For example, if you have been in a new car, it's more than likely that you'll come away with a microscopic particle of paint or

fiber sticking to you somewhere. If that particle was put under a spectrometer, the police could tell just what car you'd been in — the make, the model and even the year!

4. *Infrared sensors* are now being developed that can take "heat-pictures" of people in the dark. These sensors — really a kind of TV camera — work by photographing the invisible rays given out by the heat in our bodies. When perfected, they can be left on guard wherever valuables are stored — and will film every detail of an intruder, as plainly as if it were day (I doubt if even masks would be effective against them — although keeping your head in an ice-pack just might be!)

5. THE CASE OF THE FOUR CLUES

A recent case in England shows how a killer was caught by a spellbinding blend of science, deduction and sheer hard slogging.

The body of a strangled girl was found lying in a street. Fresh tire-tracks made the police think that she had been brought there in a car. These tire-tracks were, of course, their first "Scene of the Crime" clue. They were not content with just photographing them. Police scientists were called in, and they spent three days making plaster-of-paris molds of each track. The tracks suggested that the car was a big one, but that was all.

Then three other clues came to light. On the girl's

skirt was found a tiny flake of paint. The microscope revealed this to be made up of three separate layers of paint: a red top coat, a darker red middle coat, and a cream undercoat. These paint layers were unlike anything made in a car factory, so the police knew that the car must have been repainted by an amateur.

Next, clinging to the girl's sweater were found two tiny scraps of pale blue leather, and elsewhere — probably sticking to the heels of her shoes — were thirty red rayon fibers. The leather looked as though it had come from a car seat, obviously in very bad condition; and the red fibers must have come from a car carpet.

Real leather has not been used on car seats for years. And the makers of the car carpet, whom the police managed to contact, said that they had not made a carpet of that type for a long, long time either.

Putting these four clues together — tracks, paint, leather, fibers — the police reasoned that they had to search for a big, old red car, with peeling paint, ancient blue leather seats, and a tatty red carpet — so tatty that fibers from it came away at a touch.

These discoveries came at the start of a manhunt that went on for sixteen weeks. In the course of it, 130 detectives questioned more than 28,000 people. Fifteen hundred cars were investigated, and dozens of paint chippings and swatches of carpet were taken.

Finally, two detectives walking past a junkyard many miles from the street where the body had been found, happened to notice a large, battered *black* car lying near the top of a scrap heap. Something made them go closer. Peering in at the windows, they glimpsed pale blue leather upholstery, and tatty red carpets.

They scraped away some of the paintwork — and found underneath it traces of red, medium red, and cream. They cut away a bit of leather, and took fibers from the carpet. Then they looked around for wheels. All the wheels had been taken off the car, but they found three lying around on the heap that looked as though they might have belonged to it.

The detectives' findings were taken to a police laboratory, and compared with the original clues taken at the scene of the crime. Everything matched up perfectly — the leather, the fibers, the paint, the tire-tracks from the wheels. And finally came the clincher — if a clincher was needed. On the floor of the car was discovered a hair — exactly the shade and texture of the strangled girl's.

The police got extremely busy around that junk-yard. Everybody connected with it was questioned over and over again. And it didn't take long to discover that the car had originally belonged to a man who came from the same town as the girl. Further inquiries revealed that he had known her.

The killer had been identified at last — and his arrest soon followed.

One of the most exhaustive inquiries in the history of the police had ended successfully . . . thanks to some tire-tracks, a tiny flake of paint, an even smaller speck of leather, and thirty almost microscopic fibers.

6. BACK TO RULE ONE

You can see now why it is so important for you not to attempt to investigate any real crime on your own. Not only might it be dangerous, but anything on the scene of that crime could be a vital clue — from a fragment of broken glass to an invisible dent in the carpet.

So keep away — and do your best to see that everyone else keeps away — until the police arrive. Don't even walk on anything in the immediate area if you can help it!

Of course, I'm not saying that this crime will necessarily be important enough for the police to bring videotape cameras to the scene, or to give the carpet the laser-beam treatment, or to start sending flakes of paint for microscopic or spectrometric examination.

But one thing's certain, they'll be doing far cleverer stuff in the way of detection than could ever have been managed by the likes of you or me.

CHAPTER 10

You—Crime-Stopper

1. LOCK AND PADLOCK

The policeman who is robbed is deservedly a figure of fun. And the young detective whose personal property is stolen is equally likely to get laughs rather than sympathy from his friends.

So it's only common sense to make things difficult for a thief by following these few simple rules:

1. Lock up all the personal belongings that you can.

2. Lock your bike, if you have one.

3. Never leave valuable items — transistor radios, cassette players, pocket calculators, etc. — on top of your desk when you go to the cafeteria for lunch, or even for a few minutes during a break or recess.

4. If you keep things in a bicycle saddlebag or basket, make sure that's locked too.

5. If you're allowed to, lock your school locker.

6. Never keep dollar bills loose in the back pocket of your jeans or trousers. They can easily work their

way up and out, particularly if you play a lot of games. Use a small purse or wallet to keep them in instead. Also, get jeans with a back pocket that buttons up — and never forget to do up the button!

2. HUNT THE NUMBERS

But suppose that, in spite of everything, you do get something stolen?

You should report the theft immediately to your teacher, who will most probably contact the police.

The police will come and ask you for the fullest possible particulars of the item stolen. And here we come to a big question: *how many particulars will you be able to give them?*

Don't Look Now!

For you to have a good chance of recovering the article, they will have to know every detail. The manufacturer. The model. Any special peculiarity (e.g., bike with dent just in front of left handlebar). And — if possible — the model number and serial number.

You may not realize it, but almost everything from a cassette player to a camera, from a TV to a typewriter, has both a model number and a serial number on it somewhere — which, in these days of mass production, is just as well.

Let's say you have a bike stolen from the bike rack at school. Soon afterward, the police come across a suspect riding that very bike. But if he says that it isn't stolen, how can the police prove that it is? There may be hundreds of people riding around on bikes identical to yours at any given moment. But if you've noted down the numbers, and given them to the police, the bike can be instantly identified as yours, despite any and all denials by the thief.

Why not buy a notebook and use it for keeping a record of all your most prized possessions? The best method is to do it in eight columns — across two facing pages of the book, like this:

Item	Make	Model	Color	Size	Serial No.	Model No.	Peculiarities
RADIO	MARTINO	"ROCK STAR" VI	LIGHT RED (Fawn speaker)	5in wide x 3in high x 2in deep	X49G366	6975974	RED WRISTBAND ATTACHED

At this point, a tricky question arises. Just where does one find these serial and model numbers?

I'm afraid I can't give you a clearcut answer. The manufacturers are liable to put them in the oddest places. On a bicycle,* you're likely to find them on the seat post or stamped under the crank-case where the pedals are. On a radio, my local dealer tells me you're liable to find them either stamped on the back of the set or in the battery compartment. On a rifle or airgun, my son tells me, numbers are most likely to be on the underside, at the base of the barrel. On a typewriter (I found this one out for myself!) they are usually under the carriage. On anything else, they could be anywhere.

Streetwise

* Some bikes, I gather, have "frame numbers" — which complicate things still further!

That's why the only possible name for this section is "Hunt the Number." It sounds like a game, and that's just what finding all your model and serial numbers could turn out to be. But it's a game with a worthwhile prize: the knowledge that if anything of yours is stolen, you'll be presenting the police with a major weapon with which to beat the thief — and you'll also be doing everything possible to ensure the stolen object's swift and safe return.

3. HOME, SAFE HOME

It's natural for a young detective to appoint himself or herself Crime Prevention Officer to his or her own home.

One of the first things you should do in this capacity is to tour the house, and make sure that all the doors can be securely locked, and all the windows firmly fastened. The safest houses have locks fitted on the windows a thief is most likely to tackle, and especially good locks put on all outside doors.

These are the thief's favorite entry-points:

1. Ground-floor windows and doors.
2. Garage doors (including roll-down ones).
3. Doors leading to back gardens.
4. Second story windows — if there's a drainpipe nearby, or a flat roof a thief can stand on.

Just in case your house is burgled, you should also keep a notebook record of *family* possessions — TV sets, stereo equipment, etc. On these, the model and serial numbers shouldn't be too hard to find. These days — largely at the request of the police — manufacturers usually stamp them on the back.

Of course, there are some objects — old china, silverware, etc. — that carry entirely different identification marks. Silver has hallmarks, and fine china carries the name of the kind of ware (Doulton, Wedgwood, etc.) and usually a date.

You can't go far wrong if you examine each object carefully and put down any wording, symbols, or letters in the "Peculiarities" column in your notebook. If you've a camera with a flash, it might be an idea to photograph the most valuable pieces.

Don't think all this is a waste of time. The police rarely recover stolen objects one at a time. When they raid a thief's hideout or a shop dealing in stolen goods, they nearly always find a horde of objects, sometimes hundreds at a time, and have great difficulty returning them all to their owners.

But if you've supplied a precise description, with all possible numbers, hallmarks, and whatever, they'll have no trouble in sorting out what's yours, and returning it to you in a matter of days.

4. THE LIGHT ANSWER

But let's not be too gloomy. You don't *have* to let yourself be burgled!

The vast majority of thieves keep well clear of:

(*a*) Houses that are effectively locked up.

(*b*) Houses where they believe there may be someone at home.

Whenever all of you in the family are away from home at night, leave a light burning — preferably two lights: one on each floor of the house (then the burgler won't try and sneak in upstairs, in the belief that everyone's downstairs watching TV). Try to vary the light pattern from night to night — in case some thief is keeping your street under regular observation.

What happens if you're all going to be away for several days and nights? The best precaution is to let your neighbors know — and tell them where you can be contacted. You could even ask a neighbor to stop in and switch lights off and on.

A friend of mine was recently invited to stay for Christmas in the house of a rich businessman. As a matter of fact, he was invited to take over the house while the businessman was away on a Christmas holiday. The man had so much jewelry in the house that he was terrified of leaving the place empty.

On his first night in the house, my friend was shaken to find that as darkness fell, all the curtains in the house drew themselves; all the lights came on; and the TV and radio started blaring automatically.

This was the businessman's anti-thief system, which he had forgotten to disconnect before he went away. It just shows you what lengths some people will go

Anybody Home?

to, to keep any possible thief believing that there's somebody at home.

5. SOMEONE AT THE DOOR

There are times, though, when you *don't* want a thief to know you're home.

Suppose you happen to be alone in the house one day, and there's a suspicious knock at the door. This is a situation for which you have to prepare in advance. First, make sure that in your house, it's always possible to see who's standing outside the front door — without him or her seeing you.

You'll usually find there's a window through which you can peek. If not, tie a mirror or fix a piece of shiny tin to the end of a stick, and practice poking it out of the upstairs windows so that it slants down at the right angle to give you a view of who's at the front door.

If you hear a knock when you're alone — and if, on inspection, you don't recognize the person outside — *on no account open the door.* Just wait quietly until the person goes away.

If he or she continues to hang about on the doorstep, call up a neighbor or your parents on the phone. If you can't reach either of them, dial 911 and ask for the police.

Failing all that, go around the house noisily slamming every door in sight.

If the caller really is a would-be thief, that should have him running full speed down the street. Don't forget to whip out your crime-spotter's notebook, and (if you can manage it without him seeing you), try to get the make, color and number of his car as he drives away.

CHAPTER 11

Exercise Eye-Opener

1. BECOMING A REAL DETECTIVE

There's one question which I expect has crossed your mind a few times since you started reading this book.

How do people really become detectives?

The answer is quite simple. In ninety-nine cases out of a hundred, they begin by joining a police department.

There are some 40,000 police departments in the United States, employing some 450,000 police officers. The vast majority of them aren't detectives, though. They are uniformed patrolmen — and it is possible for a man or woman to become a police detective without spending a long time in uniform first.

Every police department has its own method of deciding which of its uniformed officers should become detectives. First they naturally look at a patrolman's record — he's unlikely to make a good detective unless he's been a good policeman in uniform.

Next he has to take an examination. A high-ranking American police officer has told me that this exam tests the same skills this book should help you develop — powers of observation and deduction. A policeman who does well on this examination is taken out of uniform and becomes what is called a "Third Detective." He can go on from there to become a Second or First Detective. Becoming a detective isn't exactly a promotion, although you do earn extra money from the start. It simply means that you become a different kind of police officer, concerned with the more interesting parts of crime-fighting: carrying out investigations, arresting major criminals, and prosecuting offenders in court. If you turn out to be good at this, you can of course receive enough promotions until you become police superintendent. (Promotion is open equally to men and women on the uniformed and detective side.)

You may decide to strike out on your own and apply for a license to operate as a private detective. In real life almost all private eyes start out with the police. But remember, you won't get anywhere, not even past those first tests, unless you have the one basic requirement of *all* detectives. You must be observant and notice things around you.

2. YOUR TRAINING STARTS HERE

That is why I am including here an "Exercise Eye-Opener" — a quiz unlike anything you have done before.

It will probably take you days to complete.

There are no answers to most of the questions — except the answers you supply yourself.

You will get no grades for doing it — except the grades you decide to award yourself.

But if you work through it, I can guarantee you one thing. You will have the sharpest pair of eyes on your street. And the chances are that you will have begun to acquire the habit of *noticing things for their own sake*.

You will, in fact, be on your way to being a very good noticer indeed.

And — I hope — a sensational young detective.

Confident Crime-Stopper

3. THE EXERCISE

NOTE. You can mark yourself any way you like, but here's a possible system. Score 2 for any question which you can answer right away, and 1 for any question where you have to go and find out the answer. There are a few questions calling for more than one answer — in these cases, the possible marks are specified.

The total possible score is somewhere between 220 and 230. If you score more than 100, you are already a pretty good detective. If you score more than 150, you can consider yourself a remarkable one. Above 200 — Scotland Yard, here you come!

There are, by the way, 100 questions, divided into ten sets of ten.

Ready? Then here we go with —

*Part One. How Well Do You Know Your Home?**

1. If there is a staircase in your house, how many steps are there on it?
2. How many chimneys are there on your roof?
3. Which room is larger — your bathroom or your kitchen?
4. How high (at its highest point) is your roof?
5. At what point does the telephone wire enter your home?

---

* Readers who live in apartments obviously can't answer Questions 1, 2, 4 or 6. So award yourselves a 6-point bonus to make up. Apartments being smaller than houses, you should be able to answer most of the other questions a lot more easily.

6. How many paces would it take a man to walk from your front gate to your front door? (A pace is roughly a yard.)

7. Where is the electric meter?

8. Where is the gas meter?

9. If you had to turn off the water, where is the stop-cock you would have to turn? (The cold-water stop-cock is the important one.)

10. How many electric outlets (for radio, lamps, TV, etc.) are there in your home?

Part Two. How Well Do You Know Your Area?

11. What are the names and occupations of the people living in the houses (or apartments) on either side of you? (Total score for this question: 8.)

12. How many houses are there on your street?

13. How many have garages?

14. Where is the nearest telephone pole?

15. How many wires are there leading from it?

16. Where is your nearest fire alarm?

17. Where is your nearest public telephone?

18. If a thief were to jump over the fence surrounding your yard, what would he be most likely to land on?

19. What is the make of the neighbor to your left's car?

20. What is the make of the neighbor to your right's car?

Part Three. How Well Do You Know Your Town?

21. Where is your town hall?

22. Where is your police station?

23. Where is your fire station?

24. What is the population of your town?

25. If you walked out of your front door, turned right, left, and right again, on what street would you be?

26. If you were flying over your town, which building would be the easiest to recognize?

27. Why?

28. What is the name of the gas station your parents most often use?

29. How many gas pumps does it have?

30. What color is the library card issued by your local library?

Part Four. How Well Do You Know Your School?

31. How many desks are there in your classroom?

32. How many people in the class have pocket calculators?

33. How many people in the class wear glasses?

34. How many teachers are there in your school?

35. How many tables are there in the school cafeteria?

36. How many exits are there in your building?

37. If you walked out of your classroom, turned right, left, left, and right again, where would you be?

38. Which teacher's handwriting is easiest to recognize?

39. Why?

40. How many notices are there — at this moment — on the nearest school bulletin-board?

Part Five. How Well Do You Know What You Read?

41. What firm publishes your favorite magazine — or comic?

42. What story (or feature) is usually on Page 2 of it?

43. What daily newspaper does your family read?

44. How much does it cost?

45. Without peeking, can you say how many chapters there are in *this* book?

46. How many books are there in your bedroom?

47. What is the oldest book you possess?

48. What is the newest?

49. Can you decode this in thirty seconds? (This question scores 4.)

    KOOBDNAH S'EVITCETED GNUOY

50. What is wrong with this SOS message?

- - - - · · - - -

Part Six. How Well Do You Know the Things You Use?

51. What make of pen are you using at present?

52. How many knobs are there on your family's TV set (front and back)?

53. What is the setting on your dial for your favorite radio station?

54. What color is your toothbrush?

55. What color is the upholstery in your family's car?

56. Whose picture is on a dime?

57. What's the label on your jeans and where is it?

58. Can you say at this moment what is in the left-hand pocket of your coat?

59. What is the wattage of the electric light bulb in your bedroom — 40, 75, 100 or 150? (If there are two bulbs, say what wattage they add up to.)

60. When you lie in bed, how many feet are you off the floor?

Part Seven. How Well Do You Know What People Look Like?

61. What color is your father's favorite tie?
62. How tall is your best friend?
63. Name someone — friend, teacher, TV actor, anyone — who has bushy eyebrows.
64. Now name someone who has a high forehead.
65. How many of your friends have round faces?
66. How many of your friends are shorter than you are?
67. What color eyes does your mother have?
68. Can you describe your own face in a sentence? (This question scores 4.)
69. Everyone's hair has a natural part. Is yours on the right side or the left?
70. Name someone with a beard, and say what kind of beard it is (goatee, full, or half). (This question scores 4.)

Part Eight. How Good Are You at Listening?

71. Which clock in your house has the loudest tick?
72. Which of your teachers has the loudest voice?
73. If your feet made a scrunching sound what could you be walking on?

74. When a whistling kettle boils, does the whistle get higher and higher or lower and lower?

75. Think of someone whose footsteps you recognize, and why those footsteps are different.

76. Which of your friends uses the word "well" most often?

77. Which of your friends says "you know" most often?

78. Which member of your family speaks most softly?

79. Does your voice sound higher or lower to you when it's on tape?

80. Which word do you use most often?

Part Nine. Can You Put Yourself on the Map?

(A policeman on his beat never walks down High Street. He "proceeds along High Street in a westerly direction." In other words, he has been trained, under all circumstances, to put himself on the map. This section — the hardest in this exercise — is designed to help you do the same. Compassless readers might like to note that if you face due west — i.e. where the sun sets in high summer — the east is behind you, the north on your right, and the south on your left.)

81. Does your front door face north, south, east or west? (A rough answer will do.)

82. Again roughly speaking, is your school north, south, east or west of your house?

83. What is the first public building (e.g., church, school, hall) you come to due east of your house?

84. Following an ancient treasure map, you walk out

of your front door, taken ten paces due east, fourteen due south and three due north. At what point would you start digging? (If it's in someone's home, garden or garage, or the middle of the street, that's too bad — but just say where it is.)

85. You wake up in the middle of the night and see a flying saucer sweep across the sky from right to left straight in front of your bedroom window. In which direction is it traveling?

86. A police car, in pursuit of a gang of thieves driving a fast Jaguar, roars past your house in a westerly direction, and the chase goes on for half a mile. Where would it wind up?

87. A dangerous maniac has escaped, and has been observed scrambling across a roof one hundred yards to the west of your home. Suppose you were the detective in charge of recapturing the man. You decide to block off the area. In which roads would you station your men? (2 points per road.)

88. What is the farthest object — apartment building, church steeple, radio tower, mountain, whatever — which you can see due north of your house?

89. If you hear a big bang, and the kitchen window of your house is shattered, in what direction was the explosion?

90. Is Chicago to the north, south, east or west of the spot where you are sitting at this moment?

Part Ten. How Well Do You Remember This Book?

(If you cannot think of an answer in this section,

you'll find it somewhere in the chapter named at the end of the question.)

91. Supposing you rushed into a phone booth, wanting to call the fire department, but you find you've no coins. What do you do? (Chapter 1.)

92. You've seen some suspicious people in a car and you want to tell the police. What four things will the police want to know about the car? (This question scores 8. Chapter 1.)

93. You want to describe a person to the police. Name three of the main things you should mention. (This question scores 6. Chapter 1.)

94. The lines *across* fingerprints are called "ridges." What are the circular lines called? (Chapter 2.)

95. How can the crook in the "Whodunit" game score 30 points? (Chapter 4.)

96. How can you tell the prints made by rubber boots from those made by shoes? (Chapter 3.)

97. In the Sherlock Holmes game, did Roger Rivers turn out to be a Yankee fan? (Chapter 4.)

98. What did secret agents traditionally make invisible ink out of? (Chapter 6.)

99. Where do you usually find the model and serial numbers on a transistor radio? (Chapter 10.)

100. What is Rule One? (Chapter 1.)

CHAPTER 12

Operation Sherlock

1. A CASE FOR YOU TO SOLVE

DON'T go away yet. Now that you've become a good observer — and, I hope, a brilliant deducer in the bargain — here's a case with quite a selection of problems for you to solve, all based on things explored earlier in this book. If you solve all the parts of the case in the times indicated, you can award yourself the title CYD1 (Champion Young Detective, First Class). If you need extra time for any of them, you're still a champion, but I'm afraid you'll lose a little class and become CYD2.

2. THE CURIOUS LETTER

Peter Davis started a Young Detectives' Club in Longfellow School, Belverdale, U.S.A. Its star member (and, incidentally, Treasurer) is a young girl named Jenny Marsden, who has — in Peter's opinion —

more brains than all the rest put together. The Long-fellow Young Detectives' Club has a deadly enemy — a group of tough boys and girls in the same school, who call themselves the Black Gang. The Black Gang is a very mysterious organization. So far the YDC hasn't even been able to discover where they hold their meetings.

One day, in middle of summer vacation, Peter Davis found a letter that had been pushed under his front door. He opened it, and saw that it was from Jenny. At first glance, it didn't make any sense what-soever.

86 Main Street,
Belverdale, 81653

Dear Peter,   July 21, 1981

Things aren't looking too black. Glad you and the gang are all okay. Will meet you soon — I hope, in no time at all. "Shed no tears, put fear behind you" as my old school motto goes! I'm not at home until round about eight or perhaps later still to-night, but after that I will phone you. Hope you'll be in.

Honestly, I'm not hiding anything, please believe that. And do try to start listening to me!

The letter ended with a scrawling signature and a row of dots and dashes, like this:

Love Jenny

— — · · ·   · · ·   · · · · 𝒥 — — · / — · ·   · ·   — —   — · — —   — · —

At second glance, of course, Peter realized that the letter contained two hidden messages — one in the words, the other in the Morse code. Grinning to himself, he deciphered the first message in 30 seconds, and the other one in 60 seconds flat.

We'll have a 90-second pause while you see if you can do the same!

3. THE URGENT PHONE CALL

Peter wasn't grinning when he'd finished deciphering.

He repeated Jenny's messages over to himself, with shivers running down his spine.

Taking every fifth word (as indicated by the underlined 5 in Jenny's zip code) the letter had read: *"Black Gang meet in shed behind school at eight tonight. Will be hiding and listening."* And the Morse P.S. had added: *"Wish me luck."*

She'll need it, Peter told himself grimly. The Black Gang contained some of the toughest kids around. And if Jenny really had discovered where they met, and was planning to hide herself and eavesdrop on one of their meetings, all alone, then she was really asking for trouble.

He rushed to the phone, and rang Jim Barnes, his second-in-command in the YDC. The phone was in a room where all the family could overhear, and so he decided to be careful.

"Hi," he said as soon as Jim came on the line. Then he burst into a fit of coughing.

"Sorry about that," he spluttered. "I'm not — you know — over my summer cold yet. Okay?"

"I think I catch the drift," said Jim meaningfully.

"M'm, yes, I hoped you would," said Peter.

"Anything more?"

"Uh-huh."

"All right. I got that too."

"Yeah . . . well . . . be seeing you."

And Peter hung up, hoping that the urgent instructions he had issued would be speedily obeyed.

Urgent instructions — to do what?

It shouldn't take you more than 30 seconds to remember!

4. THE SCRAWL ON THE WALL

Peter's cough and "Sorry about that" had told Jim that a secret message was coming. His first sentence — with a "you know" in the middle and "okay?" at the end — had told him that the YDC was holding an emergency meeting. Peter had gone on to say that the meeting would be held at the usual place ("M'm, yes") at the usual time ("Uh-huh"), and then had asked Jim to let all the others know ("Yeah . . . well").

The Longfellow YDC normally met in a locker room alongside the school tennis courts. These courts were in use all through the vacation, and so the locker room was open. Their usual meeting time was 7:30 — which, Peter reckoned, would leave just enough time for them to take some sort of action before the Black Gang assembled in that shed behind the school at 8:00.

There were five members of the Longfellow YDC, apart from Peter and Jenny. All five turned up at the locker room on time, which was pretty good, seeing that they were all on vacation and had had to come from all over town. (Though, since it had been a wet day in the middle of a rainy summer, they were probably glad of something to do.)

Peter began the meeting by reading out Jenny's letter — first the full version, then the decoded one. There were gasps and whistles of astonishment. The YDC had been trying to locate the Black Gang's meeting place for months. In discovering it, Jenny had certainly achieved a major breakthrough. But the thought of her hiding and listening in the heart of the enemy camp alarmed everyone.

Mysterious Message

"Where *can* she hide herself there, anyway?" a scholarly-looking boy named Stephen asked. "I've been over that place dozens of times. It's just a tumble-down old toolshed, belonging to the school. One time, they used to keep rakes and spades and stuff like that in there, but not anymore. The roof let in too much rain and everything got rusty. The school cleared everything out and is going to pull the whole place down, any day now. The only thing they left in there was a big white corner cupboard, where they used to keep pots and bundles of grass seed . . ." Stephen paused, then his eyes narrowed behind his thick glasses as a sudden idea struck him. "Hey, do you suppose Jenny's aiming to hide in there? There would just about be room . . ."

"She'd be crazy to try it," a rather timid girl called Angela said. "That shed's so small that the gang would be bound to hear her, if she even *breathed* too loudly!"

"All the same, I'll bet that's her plan," said Peter. "We'd better get round there as quickly as we can and stop her. The Black Gang's far too tough to play games like that with." He looked at his watch. It was already a quarter to eight, and that shed was a good five minutes' sprint away. "Let's just hope that we're not too late . . ."

Just four and a half minutes later, they arrived, breathless and panting, outside the shed. There was nobody in sight and no sound of voices. The place seemed completely deserted.

The shed door was ajar. Peter crept forward and

swung it wide open. There was nothing to be seen inside, except dust, spiderwebs, a pile of dead leaves from the previous fall . . . and the battered white cupboard where Jenny might be hiding.

With the others close behind him, Peter crossed the shed and tapped on the cupboard door.

"Jenny, you can come out. It's only us!"

There was no reply, so he tried the door. It opened at his touch.

The cupboard was as bare as Mother Hubbard's . . . but on the floor, lying in a crumpled heap, was a raincoat which looked like Jenny's. Peter was about to pick it up, when suddenly some letters scrawled on the cupboard wall caught his eye. It was quite a long message from Jenny — in the Longfellow YDC code.

LAPAN! PDA CWJC IAP WP
ORRAJ. JKP AECDP. PDAU
YWQCDP IA WJZ DWRA
ODQP IA EJ DANA. PDAU
WNA PWHGEJC WXKQP
GEZJWLLEJC IA

Peter got out his notebook, and wrote down two alphabets, one underneath the other. The second alphabet was a certain number of spaces along from the first. With this in front of him, he deciphered the message in three minutes.

It was easy for him, of course. He knew the correct number of spaces to move the bottom alphabet. But even if he hadn't, he could have worked it out, using the Young Detective Code-breaking System.

In, say, eight to ten minutes — can you?

5. THE RIPPED RAINCOAT

As soon as he had decoded Jenny's message, Peter read it aloud to the others. He couldn't keep his voice from shaking slightly as he did so.

" *'Peter,'* " he read, " " *'the gang met at seven, not eight. They caught me and have shut me in here. They are talking about kidnapping me* —' "

He stopped.

"Well, go on," said Angela.

"Afraid I can't. There isn't any more. The message ends there — and I don't like the *way* it ends at all. The last letter trails off, almost as if Jenny had been seized and dragged away."

Stephen's eyes narrowed behind his glasses, as they always did when he was scared or puzzled. At that moment, he was obviously both.

"I can't see Jenny letting herself be grabbed, even by the Black Gang, without putting up a fight. But there's no sign of a struggle. No marks of scuffling in the dust, for instance, or —"

He broke off, as Peter picked up the raincoat and held it out. There were long tears in at least three places, and one sleeve had very nearly been ripped clean away.

"There are your signs of struggle," Peter said. "It looks as though she fought so hard to get away that this was snatched right off her, and completely ruined in the bargain. Which shows once again that the Black Gang isn't exactly fun to play games with."

There was a tense, angry pause. Then George, the toughest and bravest member of the Longfellow YDC, murmured softly:

"They won't find *us* fun to play games with either, you can take it from me!"

This was greeted with a roar of approval, but Peter didn't join in. With the clue-hunting instinct of the born young detective, he had started to turn out the pockets of the raincoat — and was staring thoughtfully at the odd collection of objects this produced.

There were six items in all.

From the left-hand pocket had come:

1. An old library card with the name "Miss Jennifer Marsden" typed on it. (That meant beyond doubt that the raincoat was Jenny's.)

2. A faded, broken tortoiseshell comb, with a strand of hair still attached to one of its few remaining teeth. (Peter didn't have his magnifying glass with him, but the hair was dark, the same color as Jenny's.)

3. A small piece of chocolate, not wrapped in any kind of paper, and almost literally as hard as a rock.

From the right-hand pocket had come:

1. Half of a return bus ticket to High Ridge, a small town twenty miles north of Belverdale. It was dated June 2, 1980, and had cost $1.50.

2. A dusty piece of ribbon, about three inches long, and knotted in four places. (Jenny, Peter remembered, always wore ribbons to match her outfits.)

3. A crumpled card giving the 1980 Longfellow tennis schedule for "May thru July." (Jenny was crazy about tennis and most other sports.)

Peter stared down at the objects for quite a while.

"There's something strange about these," he said, almost to himself. "Something very strange indeed . . ."

You have five minutes to work out why. And — in case you'd like an extra clue — you might have to turn back to the start of the chapter before you can.

Up for Ransom

6. THE RANSOM NOTE

Peter was still staring down at the collection of objects when suddenly there was a yell from Stephen. He had been taking a look around outside the shed, and had found a ransom note stuck in a large flowerpot standing on the grass just by the door.

The note was written in crude capitals, and read:

Get THIS Y.D.S! WE HAVE TAKEN YOUR LOUSY SPY. IF YOU WANT HER BACK SAFE, IT'LL COST YOU $20. PUT THE MONEY IN THIS POT. THEN GO BACK TO YOUR "SECRET" H.Q. (THE TENNIS LOCKER ROOM, ISN'T IT? SEE? WE KNOW EVERYTHING) AND STAY THERE FOR 40 MINUTES WHILE WE TAKE THE MONEY AND RETURN THE GOODS. IF YOU KEEP WATCH OR LAY TRAPS OR TRY TO CHEAT US IN ANY WAY, IT'LL BE BAD FOR JENNY ... VERY BAD INDEED.

THE BLACK GANG

"Twenty dollars!" Stephen's eyes were narrowing again. "Heck. Can we raise that kind of money — just like that?"

The young detectives turned out their pockets, and found that they could, although it would leave all six of them cleaned out for the rest of the day, and in the case of two or three unfortunates, for the rest of the week.

The thought of that ripped raincoat, though, was enough to silence all argument. Dollar bills, quarters pennies, and dimes rained into the pot, and the required ransom was reached in under a minute.

There were no arguments, either about carrying out the gang's instructions to the letter.

Even the belligerent George had to admit: "They've got us where they want us — as long as they've got Jenny!"

Peter, though, didn't have anything to say.

He had spotted something about that ransom note — something so odd that it left him thinking furiously.

If *you* start thinking furiously, in about 60 seconds, you should have spotted it too!

7. END OF THE CASE

Feeling beaten and very, very angry, the six members of the Longfellow YDC walked back to their HQ. They stayed inside it for exactly forty minutes, by Peter's brand-new digital watch. Then they burst out and sprinted back to the shed.

Nothing seemed to have changed there, at first. But when they looked in the flowerpot, they saw that the $20 had gone; and when they entered the shed, they heard a banging noise coming from the white cupboard.

They opened the door, and there were gasps of relief. There, in front of them, stood Jenny — a very untidy-looking Jenny. (Apparently, she had been unceremoniously dumped in the cupboard in a sack a few minutes before, and the banging noise they had heard was her climbing out of it.) Her dark hair was covered with dust. Her face was pale; her eyes were wild. But she seemed to be otherwise quite unharmed.

"Glad to have you back," said Peter quietly.

He paused, and then added, by no means so quietly:

"And we'd also be glad to have that twenty dollars back — which you stole from us, your own friends, by the meanest, sneakiest trick I've ever seen!"

A shock wave of amazement and disbelief swept around the whole group. Jenny just stood, open-mouthed, staring as Peter continued, his words now lashing her with the force of hailstones:

"Admit it. You faked that story about the Black Gang meeting, the kidnapping — everything! You knew that when I got that letter, I'd be bound to call an emergency meeting, and that we'd all come rushing down to this shed to stop you from putting yourself in danger. You left that message on the cupboard wall — and that raincoat, ripped to pieces on the floor — to make us think you'd been seized after a terrible fight. You also faked the ransom note. All the time we were reading it, and emptying our pockets to save you from an awful fate, you were hiding somewhere close by, laughing at us, and waiting for our twenty dollars to drop into your lap!"

Jenny didn't attempt to deny anything that Peter was saying. She just folded her arms, and stared back, half-sulky, half-defiant.

She was still holding the sack in which she claimed to have been tied up. But everyone suddenly noticed that there was no sign of any string . . .

"Very clever of you, Peter," Jenny finally said. "You surely do deserve to be leader of our club! What gave me away?"

"The things in the raincoat pockets made me suspicious at first," Peter replied. "It was obviously your raincoat. There was a library card with your name on it; a comb with strands of dark hair, just your color, and a piece of ribbon with knots in it — I knew how you liked to wear ribbons in your hair. But although it was obviously yours, it looked as if you hadn't been using that coat for a very long time. The comb was faded, and had hardly any teeth left. There was a lump of chocolate, hard as a rock. Chocolate doesn't go rock hard, and combs don't get in that state, unless they've been left around for months and months. And there were two items — a bus ticket and a tennis schedule — dating from way back last summer — 1980!* Now *this* summer has been a very rainy one. You'd have used that coat a lot if it had been a new one, and would certainly have cleared a

* How, you may ask, can the reader be expected to know that all this is happening in the summer of 1981? The answer is: from the date — July 21, 1981 — at the top of Jenny's letter to Peter, at the start of this chapter. I advised you to look back there and see!

lot of that old stuff out of the pockets. Therefore —
this was an old coat, probably ready for the trash,
which you'd got out of the attic, especially for this
evening's fun and games. Now why should you have
done that? Obviously because you *intended to rip
it up!*"

"That doesn't necessarily follow," said Jenny. "My
new coat might have gone to the cleaner's, and I
might have gotten the old one out to use while it was
away."

"True," said Peter. "I said that the things in the
pocket only aroused my suspicions. They didn't
amount to proof positive against you."

"Then what did?"

"A little mistake you made at the end of that ransom note," Peter said. "You were careful to use block
capitals almost the whole way through — but when
you came to your own name, you forgot, and wrote
"Jenny" like you always do, with the *J joined onto
the E* with a special flourish.* You could almost say
that you signed that note yourself — in your own
handwriting!"

There were gasps of astonishment and admiration
all round.

"Well?" Peter finished grimly. "Can we have our
twenty dollars back now, please?"

But for the Longfellow YDC, there was more
astonishment to come.

"Not on your life," said Jenny, with a cold glare

* See Jenny's letter at start of chapter.

Admit it! You Did It!

around at them all. "Aren't you forgetting a few things? I'm your Treasurer. And there's the little matter of a twenty-dollar tape recorder I bought on behalf of the club at the end of last term. I seem to remember that you each promised to chip in and to mail the money to me during the first week of the vacation. But six weeks have gone by, and I haven't received a single measly cent from any of you. And since I was pretty low financially, I thought this might be a good way of — er — balancing our books. Well, Longfellow YDC?" she ended defiantly. "What have you brilliant brains to say to that?"

Nobody, in fact, had much to say for quite a while. Then Peter, thrusting his hands deep into his painfully empty pockets, managed a slow, rueful grin.

"I vote that we accept our Treasurer's report," he said faintly, "and close this meeting — and the case."

Operation Sherlock had been an Exercise Eye-Opener for them all.

Notes

Notes

Notes